HOWARD S. BECKER

Who is Howard S. Becker? This book traces his career, examining his work and contributions to the field of sociology. Themes covered include Becker's theoretical conceptualizations, approaches, teaching style, and positioning in the intellectual milieu. Translated from French by sociologist Robert Dingwall, the English edition benefits from an editorial introduction and additional referencing, as well as a new foreword by Becker himself.

Jean Peneff is Emeritus Professor of Sociology at the University of Aix-Marseille, France. He has played a leading role in introducing qualitative research methods to French sociology, pioneering the use of participant observation.

Robert Dingwall is a consulting sociologist and part-time professor of sociology at Nottingham Trent University, UK. He has written widely on law, medicine, science, and technology, focusing on professions, work, organizations and interaction, and on research methods and ethics.

Praise for this book

"Howard Becker's long and distinguished career receives a welcome and engaging review. Peneff's book, in Dingwall's translation, more than does justice to Becker's clarity of thought and expression. The modesty of Becker's claims is matched only by the scale of his achievements. The reception of Becker's sociology in France is a particularly intriguing aspect of the book and of his contribution to sociological reasoning more widely."

Paul Atkinson, *Cardiff University*

"Peneff suggests intriguing insights into the work of Howard Becker through his lens as a French sociologist. He encourages the reader to think more broadly and in depth about Becker's work and to question some of our assumptions about French sociology. Extensive quotes from Becker's interviews may be unfamiliar to many readers, further illuminating his contributions to sociology."

Ruth Horowitz, *New York University*

"Peneff provides an original and comprehensive appreciation of Howard Becker's work conducted over more than 50 years examining the processes and interactions that mark everyday life in a variety of social worlds. An important study for qualitative researchers and for all those working in the spirit of classic Chicago sociology!"

Bob Emerson, *University of California, Los Angeles*

HOWARD S. BECKER

Sociology and Music in the Chicago School

Jean Peneff

Translated by Robert Dingwall

Routledge
Taylor & Francis Group

NEW YORK AND LONDON

English edition published 2018
by Routledge
711 Third Avenue, New York, NY 10017

and by Routledge
2 Park Square, Milton Park, Abingdon, Oxon OX14 4RN

This English edition © 2018 Taylor & Francis

Foreword © 2018 Howard S. Becker

Routledge is an imprint of the Taylor & Francis Group, an informa business

First published in French by Editions L'Harmattan 2014

Library of Congress Cataloging-in-Publication Data
Names: Peneff, Jean, author.
Title: Howard S. Becker : sociology and music in the Chicago School /
Jean Peneff ; translated by Robert Dingwall.
Other titles: Howard S. Becker. English
Description: New York, NY : Routledge, 2018. | "First published in French 2014: Howard S. Becker, Paris: Editions L'Harmattan." | Includes bibliographical references and index.
Identifiers: LCCN 2018007941 (print) | LCCN 2018009523 (ebook) |
ISBN 9780429467752 (eBook) ISBN 9781629583143 (hardback : alk. paper) |
ISBN 9781629583150 (pbk. : alk. paper) | ISBN 9780429467752 (ebook : alk. paper)
Subjects: LCSH: Becker, Howard Saul, 1928- | Chicago school of sociology. Sociology.
Classification: LCC HM479.B435 (ebook) | LCC HM479.B435 P46 2018 (print) | DDC 301--dc23
LC record available at https://lccn.loc.gov/2018007941

ISBN: 978-1-62958-314-3 (hbk)
ISBN: 978-1-62958-315-0 (pbk)
ISBN: 978-0-429-46775-2 (ebk)

Typeset in Bembo
by Taylor & Francis Books

CONTENTS

FOREWORD

Howard S. Becker

It is a great pleasure to introduce Jean Peneff's book about my intellectual career and adventures. I had already been "in the business" of sociology for many years when I met Jean. He was one of the members of the "École de Chicago de Paris," the other members being Jean-Pierre Briand, Henri Peretz, and Jean-Michel Chapoulie who, as their nickname suggested, were great devotees of Robert E. Park, William I.Thomas and all the other legendary members of that generation of Chicago sociology.

Peneff was distinctive in this crew by being a Gascon – like d'Artagnan in Dumas' novel (*The Three Musketeers*) – youthful, impulsive and on occasion brilliant, as this book proves. Naturally, he discerned similar virtues in me and in the sociological work I did. I wasn't such a heroic figure, but my inborn rebelliousness shaped my approach to teaching. I think that nothing proved to him our intellectual kinship more than the "special classroom" I taught my field work class in, one that I had persuaded the provost of Northwestern University to have constructed to my specifications (though it took no real construction). Anyone who has seen a standard French or American classroom finds it easy to understand my intention immediately. The American classroom has seats or benches bolted to the floor. The French version, the "amphi," is even worse: a large hall, of long, curved desks with benches, from which the students have an unobstructed view of the distant figure who delivers wisdom for them to write down in their notebooks. Teachers can't have a conversation with people whose surroundings separate them in that way.

My request to the authorities for my "special innovative classroom" was as far as you could get from that. I wanted the room separated from other classrooms – and so I got a room that hadn't, from the look of things, been used for anything much for many years, in the basement of one of the oldest buildings on the Northwestern campus. The only other room down there was a large toilet facility for men. And there was a coffee machine! The room's darkness – the only windows were toward the front of one of the walls where they let a little sun in – satisfied another of my conditions, by allowing the room to be darkened so that films and slides could be projected. Finally, any built-in or other existing furniture (desks, chairs, etc.) would be removed.

The final, and most important part, of the request was for $200 that I could spend for furniture at the nearby Salvation Army store (stipulating that no purchasing department bureaucrats would be involved, I would do the purchasing myself). I happily went furniture shopping and got a lot for my money – a wonderful broken down sofa, some scattered more or less wrecked chairs, no tables or desks. A handful of falling apart cushions you could use for sitting on the floor as back rests or whatever else came to mind.

The first day of the first class I was purposely late. I wanted to see how they would solve the mystery of the where the teacher would sit. No obvious clue indicated where that should be so, in the end, the students as they entered just sat wherever. When I finally arrived I chose a spot from those they had left. (On the following days I more or less systematically sat in a different place for each session, until they realized that there really was no place reserved for the teacher.)

Then the first class began and I explained that this was a class and their assignment was to pick something *and* someplace to do their research on, go there and stay for four or more hours, and then go home and write down everything they'd seen and heard and turn that in at the next class (class met twice a week). Objections rose on every side. They couldn't make such an important decision so quickly, they weren't ready yet. I overruled that complaint, agreeing that they weren't ready yet, but explaining that they would never be ready to make such a decision, that that wasn't how the most important research problems (or any research problems) were decided.

I decided to put down rebellion immediately, explaining that I was inflexible on this point, I would not let anyone leave the room without telling us all what they were going to do, who and where they were going to observe. I thought I'd only get away with this shock tactic the first year, but it always worked. Either the older students kept this surprise to themselves or, knowing it was coming, didn't help the newcomers prepare.

So, in the end, everyone named a place and learned quickly that I wouldn't let them have a week or two to get ready, that the clock was already running.

The second day I sat in a different place and collected papers. A few tried to tell me that they didn't have "enough," I insisted on taking whatever notes they did have. And then said that I would read and comment on them before the next class. Which I did. I held myself to the same standards I held them to. But I didn't then go on to a critique of what they had done. Instead, I asked someone about some common difficulty that had cropped up in her notes, asked her about some aspect of it so that we all got a better idea of what had actually happened, tried to strip away any "technical" language that could obscure who had done what and said what. And then asked if anyone else had a similar problem which of course, someone had, and soon, no surprise because, after all, I had read all this stuff already when I read their notes.

The students learned a lot from this quotidian exercise: what you could extract from student exercises when they were accurately reported, for instance, the daily craft of field work and, at the same time, the reality that lies behind the big scary language of Social Theory.

It went off like that from day to day, twice a week, and gradually the students learned to talk directly to each other without me having to suggest that they do that when there was something pertinent to both their projects that they could see. As a result, ten or fifteen minutes or more could go by without me saying a word, and the class conversation took on a life of its own, whose direction I neither had to nor could direct – I was reprimanded more than once for trying to do that. I was happy. And they were learning, and knew it. (As a result, of course, Jean Peneff knew it too.)

There were a few extraordinary occasions when students insisted on me intervening. One of my most vivid memories (Peneff was not, unfortunately, there to share it) took place when Betty took advantage of a quiet moment to say, in a hurt and aggrieved tone, "It's not fair!" I asked, of course, what wasn't fair, and she repeated, "It's not fair! All the boys get to study things like the fire station or the police station and the girls have to study day care centers and nursery schools." Betty herself had chosen a nursery school.

I let the moment of silence that followed go on, and then said, "Did I tell you you had to do that?" and let the silence resume. Everyone felt the moment's heaviness. Finally she said no, I hadn't said she or anyone else had to choose whatever they had chosen, but still . . . . The weight of that unspoken "still" hung there for a long while. I certainly had nothing to add to such a self-evident point.

But finally I broke the ice by naming the enemy – our unquestioned acceptance of what "they," all those other vague people who were littering our imaginations, thought we should be doing. Which led quickly to discussing what terrible results would occur if we didn't do what "they" wanted, and once you let that topic come up it was all over. They realized that no fearful consequence would follow, they really were free to indulge their wildest dreams because the worst that could happen was that they would learn that the worst was true – e.g., that very exciting things almost never happen in a fire station, it's most of the time a boring job. But whether that was true or not had nothing to do with Betty being a girl or Tom being a boy.

So the big lesson of that day arose of its own accord. The only way you could make that point to a class was by waiting until they stumbled across it in their own wanderings. It's a lesson you can't plan, you just wait for the occasion to present itself and grab it when it shows up.

Peneff, an alert observer and participant, quickly got into the swing of the class and was soon contributing from his stock of experiences. I've learned lot from what he has to say and so will you.

Howie Becker
San Francisco
February 2018

INTRODUCTION TO THE ENGLISH EDITION

Robert Dingwall

At one level, this is a book about Howard Becker and his contributions to sociology over the last seventy years. Jean Peneff is presenting Becker's scholarship to students and colleagues in the French-speaking world. In particular, he wants to promote interest in Becker's work beyond the writings on deviance, for which he is best known in France, and elsewhere. The choices of translators and publishers have obscured Becker's other contributions – to the sociology of work and occupations, to the sociology of art and culture, and to method and methodology. Through this discussion, however, Peneff also pursues two other agendas, both of which have a much wider international resonance for sociology. One is a critique of the work and influence of Pierre Bourdieu, whose writings have been much in vogue throughout the anglophone world for the last two decades or so.[1] The other, which follows from the analysis of Bourdieu, sets out a position on the relationship between sociology and society. Becker, Peneff argues, offers an alternative to the currently fashionable program of "public sociology." These themes are more implicit. As you read this book, you need to ask what contrast is implied at the moments where Peneff endorses or praises Becker's arguments. Who or what is the "other" that is being put down?

This introduction will help you with that reading. It is organized into three sections. The first sketches the context of French sociology within which the original was written. What does this look like from the inside? The second examines the way in which Becker's work, and that of the Chicago School more generally, has been used to challenge certain styles of sociological thinking, represented by Bourdieu, that are by no means exclusive to France. What has made Becker such an attractive figure to a substantial group of French sociologists? Why should sociologists, globally, take notice of this? The third section looks at what it means to act in the world as a sociologist. How should sociologists, anywhere, relate to other citizens, and to the societies in which they are embedded?

There is, of course, something slightly perverse about this discussion: one of the things that Peneff finds particularly attractive about Becker is his refusal to take positions or directly challenge other sociologists. As Peneff notes, Becker generally confines himself to offering up his own work and inviting his readers to make of it what they will. On the other hand, Becker can do this on the basis of wide reading and extensive scholarship. Those of us whose lives and careers have followed different courses may need a more explicit context to fully appreciate what is being placed in front of us.

French Sociology: Myths and Realities

For most anglophone readers, the first thing to understand is that much of what you think you know about French sociology is wrong. We suffer as much from the vagaries of translation as do our French colleagues. If you read the accounts of the recent history of French sociology produced by the French themselves, you will find few mentions of Michel Foucault, Jacques Derrida, Jean-François Lyotard, Gilles Deleuze, Hélène Cixous, Julia Kristeva, Luce Irigaray and many others associated with the contemporary reception of French thought in anglophone sociology. These writers may be linked to developments in the history of ideas, of literary and cultural studies, or of philosophy – but they are not everyday currency in French sociology. The only major scholars whose work can genuinely be said to be shared between anglophone and francophone sociological communities are Pierre Bourdieu and, to some extent, Bruno Latour. We will come back to Latour later. For the moment, it is important to note that current French sociology is defined less by Bourdieu than by the reaction to Bourdieu. As Peneff notes, Bourdieu is a polarizing figure, both as a scholar and as a professional role model, a view echoed by Alain Touraine in commenting on Bourdieu's death: "He was an unavoidable point of reference, both positive and negative" (Rousset 2018). To the south and west of the country, according to Peneff, Bourdieu's legacy still dominates in departments of sociology. In the north and east, and in Paris itself, sociologists have taken their inspiration from the US traditions represented by Becker's work to develop an alternative. Peneff overgeneralizes a little – Becker has fans in Bordeaux, Bourdieu has left an imprint on Paris and there are other alternatives. The key point, though, is that Bourdieu has not been the hot ticket in France over the period in which he has been enthusiastically embraced by the anglophone world.

The rise and decline of Bourdieu's influence reflects the changing social, political and institutional context of French sociology – and its relations with US sociology. In the anglophone world, we have bound the history of French sociology into our own origin myths. Durkheim is an iconic figure for us, central to our own canon. He was a great and original scholar – but his institution-building project for sociology failed, when his most talented students, including his own son, were killed in World War I. Durkheim himself died in 1917. His contemporaries attributed this to a broken heart.[2] The survivors were divided and less engaged with the administrative and organizational challenges of building a discipline. There were two chairs and four recognized university positions in sociology in 1910: only a handful of new posts had been created by 1950. At that date, fewer than a dozen courses were labeled as sociology and there was no national examination: sociology could only be studied in universities as a subordinate element of philosophy. The situation was little better in respect of research. This attracted minimal public funding between the two World Wars, private funding dried up as a result of the economic crisis of the 1920s, and the Rockefeller Foundation concluded that Germany and the UK were better locations to invest in research on social policy. An upturn began in the late 1930s, with a new generation of researchers, like Jean Stoetzel, influenced by US developments in opinion polling and social surveys. This, however, was cut short by the outbreak of World War II. Some post-war leaders, like Georges Gurvitch and Raymond Aron, went into exile. An older generation, like Marcel Mauss and Maurice Halbwachs, remained and suffered serious persecution: Halbwachs died in a concentration camp. Others, like Stoetzel, worked with the Vichy government on statistical and survey studies. Where courses survived, Durkheim's secular and socialist approach gave way to conservative, Catholic moralizing (Masson 2008; Masson and Schrecker 2016).

Durkheim's legacy was a sociology that was relatively indifferent to developments outside France. Coming from the border town of Strasbourg, he read and spoke German and studied there for several months in 1886 (Fournier 2013, pp. 70–83). He also drew extensively on English writers like Herbert Spencer, J. S Mill and Thomas Hobbes (see also Turner 1984). However, by 1900, most of these authors were no longer acknowledged and he was insisting on the distinctively French character of the sociological tradition that he was creating. It has been suggested that this was partly a fall-out from the Dreyfus affair and the need for someone with a Jewish background to make a conspicuous show of patriotism (Mosbah-Natanson 2008).[3] Although Durkheim lectured on pragmatism in 1913–1914, he does not seem to have had much time for US sociology. The feeling appears to have been mutual: Albion Small, the founding department chair (1892–1926) at Chicago reviewed his work rather coolly (Fournier 2013, p. 471) and the influential Chicago textbook edited by Robert Park and Ernest Burgess (1921) only included two small extracts from his writings. Although both Mauss and Halbwachs, his main intellectual heirs, visited the US between the two world wars, neither made much of an impression, nor seems to have taken much benefit from the contact. Halbwachs spent three months in the Chicago sociology department in 1930. However, he thought it was profoundly "stupid" of Burgess to suggest that he should "go to a spot where one might come across murderers and was content to see the city of Chicago from the outside, passing through its streets and markets like a tourist" (Chapoulie 2008, p. 229).[4] British and German sociologists appear to have been equally unimpressed by Durkheim (Studholme 1995; Fitzi and Marcucci 2017). It was only with the publication of Talcott Parsons's (1937) *The Structure of Social Action*, that Durkheim acquired the canonical status that he now has. Even in France, his reputation was uncertain until Raymond Aron (1967) performed a similar task in *Les Étapes de la Pensée Sociologique*, based on a course of lectures that he had been giving at the Sorbonne.

When French sociology was reconstructed after World War II, it rested on very flimsy foundations. There were only two professors authorized to supervise graduate degrees – Gurvitch and Georges Davy, Durkheim's last surviving student. Aron and Stoetzel did not acquire this status until 1955. In terms of institution-building, arguably the most important figure was Georges Friedmann at the *École Pratique des Hautes Études*, who attracted a number of graduate students and junior researchers with interests in the sociology of work. The best known outside France are Michel Crozier and Alain Touraine. Many of Friedmann's students had backgrounds in the Communist elements of the Resistance, as did Friedmann himself, although he had been drifting away from the Party since the late 1930s (Chapoulie 1991, pp. 333–334; Masson and Schrecker 2016, pp. 33–34). In a small way, French sociology became part of the Cold War struggle for ideological dominance with investments from US foundations and agencies, and from liberal interests in France. In reality, the French Communist party was unsupportive of sociological inquiries, which were seen as potentially contesting its claim to be the voice of the working class (Drouard 1982).[5] The US funding promoted links with US universities, particularly on the East Coast, where sociologists had been much more closely engaged with the government during World War II (Gerhardt 1999; Mandler 2013). Chicago was less involved, although Peneff mentions Paule Verdet, who did a PhD there with Everett Hughes in the late 1940s. However, Verdet remained in the US, where she made a successful academic career (Verdet 1997). Masson and Schrecker (2016, p. 34) also note a visit in 1950 by Henri Mendras, who worked with both Gurvitch and Friedmann. Chicago urban ecology made a particular impact on Paul-Henri Chombart de Lauwe (Chombart de Lauwe and Bertin 1952), who published a study of Paris based on Burgess's model of cities as concentric rings around a central core.

French sociology in the 1950s was a small-scale and institutionally marginal enterprise. Its relationship to the US was ambivalent. The Americans were envied for the way in which their society recognized their intellectual legitimacy. This meant that they could engage with policy communities in and around government, from which French sociologists were largely excluded. The French state was committed to social planning in ways that strongly favored economics over sociology, except for opinion polling. However, like many European scholars, French sociologists tended to be critical of the political compromises made by the Americans in exchange for their public profile. Where was the radical edge of US sociology? Where was the concern for social justice and the working class? Although there was some qualitative research being done in France, this was in the shadow of anthropology and generated little in the way of systematic reflections on method or methodology. By the end of the decade, there were still fewer than 100 sociologists working in research and no more than twenty-five teaching on university courses (Masson and Schrecker 2016, p. 40). The first sociology undergraduate degrees only began in 1958, in Paris and Bordeaux.[6]

At the beginning of the 1960s, there was a shift in the institutional environment. French government planners became concerned about the potential mismatch between economic and social modernization (Berrebi-Hoffmann and Grémion 2009, pp. 42–43). Sociology was now seen as a useful resource for understanding societal adaptation to technical change and promoting industrial productivity, while being concerned to meet the human needs of citizens. Investment in sociology was a way to understand, manage, and contain potential social conflict. This produced a wave of national research contracts and support for a rapid expansion of sociology degree courses (Masson and Schrecker 2016, pp. 44–46). As in the UK, there was a sudden demand for university teachers that could only be met by appointing people from neighboring disciplines. In the French context, this meant a strong continuing influence from philosophy and, to a lesser extent, social psychology and anthropology. These influences became embedded in the structures and reward systems of the discipline and are, in many ways, personified by Bourdieu, although he was not unique in this respect. His career began with studies in philosophy and then moved into structural approaches to anthropology and linguistics, as represented by Claude Lévi-Strauss. Crozier also had a philosophical background and the pattern continues with a more contemporary scholar like Latour. The dominance of theoretical studies in university teaching was, though, somewhat at odds with the expectation of the funders that the expansion of courses would produce a cadre of graduates competent to undertake polls and surveys to inform national decision-making. This style of work was best represented by Raymond Boudon. While he had also started out as a philosopher, he had moved to the US and worked with Paul Lazarsfeld, before returning to promote a view of sociology as the quantitative study of social facts. Bourdieu and Boudon both contributed to the revival of interest in Durkheim, but emphasized very different aspects of his thought. Bourdieu took up the parts of Durkheim's (1995) thought, particularly from *Elementary Forms of Religious Life*, which had been revived by Lévi-Strauss in the search for deep structures that shaped human thought and action. Boudon followed the program of *Rules of Sociological Method* and Durkheim's (1938) attempt to identify "social facts."

Given its sponsors' hopes that sociology would contribute to the management of social conflict, French sociology was badly affected by *les évenements* of May 1968.[7] While the older generation of professors mostly thought of themselves as leftists, they were criticized for their conservatism by a younger generation. The professoriate reacted in different ways to this challenge. The result was a series of quarrels and ruptures that broke up the discipline's leadership for a generation. France did not, for example, have a fully functioning and inclusive national sociological association until 2002. Some leaders, like Aron, Crozier, and Touraine spoke out against the disruption. Crozier left his university post after 1968 and concentrated on his CNRS position, doing organizational research and consultancy for socialist governments under the presidency (1981–1995) of François Mitterrand (Crozier 2005, p. 7; Masson 2008, p. 70). A few, like Henri Lefebvre (1969), maintained their affiliations with the orthodox Marxism of the French Communist

Party. Others, like Claude Dubar eventually abandoned the Communist connection – Dubar resigned from the party in 1983, becoming one of the promoters of the liberal alternative offered by the Chicago tradition and making an important contribution to the foundation of the *Association Française de Sociologie* (Demazière 2015). Although his study of cultural exclusion, *Les Héritiers* (Bourdieu and Passeron 1964), has often been considered a key text for understanding May 1968, Bourdieu always remained silent on his response to those events. Grémion (2005) suggests that this was convenient, in that it allowed him to be seen as both for and against, depending upon the context. Advocates of the democratization of universities could take his published work as an inspiration while he remained privately aligned with the establishment critics of the disruption.

Bourdieu secured the key position of professor of sociology at the *Collège de France* in 1982, which he occupied until shortly before his death in 2002.[8] Such posts are filled through election by the Collège's Assembly of Professors, which means that success often depends on the ability to network and promote oneself to people outside one's own discipline. Peneff notes that many people thought that Alain Touraine was a more worthy candidate but that he lacked the motivation to lobby on his own behalf.[9] In a country where government is highly centralized and the higher education and research system has a strong status hierarchy, such posts offer considerable opportunities for patronage and the promotion of one's preferred people and orthodoxies.[10] Peneff speaks for many French sociologists in criticizing the ruthlessness with which Bourdieu used the privileges of his position to advance careers and, in particular, to present his version of sociology in the media and other public fora as *the* version of sociology. Crozier was also critical, as in this interview (Crozier 2005, pp. 7–8; see also Masson 2008, p. 70):[11]

> Crozier: ..the wider public interested in the social sciences has been patiently colonized by Pierre Bourdieu, and his collaborators, with an anti-establishment perspective. Thanks to his influence with the newspaper, *Le Monde*, he has managed to impose his model on the whole of sociology.
> Interviewer: Do you think that sociology is more and more turning in on itself so that we are seeing an increasing disconnection between the discipline and the wider public?
> Crozier: Yes and no. Certainly this self-isolation, which plagues French society, has got worse. Debate has ceased. But, at the same time, it has created the orthodoxy of denunciation, which I have just summarized. These people are the puppets of the system. They may strip away the veils from reality – but they do not offer any clues about how to understand it, let alone transform it. We have gone back to the most basic Marxism, even if the citations to Marx and the revolution have disappeared.

Bourdieu's stance was seen to be predominantly negative and critical, focused on denouncing the errors and failings of other social actors, while lacking a positive vision of his own. To the extent that there is an implied utopia in Bourdieu's thought, there is no pathway to achieving it, only a reflex to criticize the imperfections of the routes actually being pursued. In fairness, Bourdieu is not the only sociologist to be guilty of these sins but his high public profile made them particularly visible.

From the early 1980s onwards, resistance to Bourdieu began to become more evident. This took a number of forms, of which one was the discovery of US qualitative traditions in sociology by people like Peneff, Jean-Michel Chapoulie, and Henri Peretz. While these were not entirely unknown, as noted above, US sociology had been very much identified with functionalism, survey methods, and political conservatism. Initially, as in the UK, the distinctions within US qualitative sociology were not well recognized: Alain Coulon, for example, published introductory texts on ethnomethodology (1987) and the Chicago School (1992) that tended to present them as part of a single project. Although some of Goffman's work (1968, 1973, 1975) had been translated for a series edited by Bourdieu in the late 1960s and early 1970s,[12] most of the classic interactionist studies did not appear in French until the mid-1980s: Eliot Freidson's *Profession of Medicine* was translated in 1984 and Becker's *Outsiders* in 1985, for example. Quoting Chapoulie (2001), Masson (2008, pp. 184–185; see also Masson and Schrecker 2016, pp. 62–63) notes how the lingering influence of philosophy had distorted sociology's scale of intellectual values, prioritizing abstract generalization over empirical knowledge. However a measure of decentralization in government created new funding opportunities for projects at regional and local levels where it was less clear that large-scale survey methods were appropriate. Many of these were focused on the challenges of urban living and of responses to mass immigration: the Chicago experience offered direct models for such studies.[13] As Masson notes, though, the main areas of influence were in the study of professions, work and organizations, particularly in health care (e.g. Peneff 1992), and in studies of culture: Becker's approach to the sociology of art was directly contrasted with that of Bourdieu. I will return to this in the next section, but it is worth noting, with Masson, that there was very little translation of writings about field methods. W.F. Whyte's (1943) *Street Corner Society* was not translated until 1996, for example. *The Discovery of Grounded Theory* by Glaser and Strauss (1967) only appeared in French in 2010. Becker's own late career writings on method were translated more promptly, but only after 2000. Nevertheless, by 1998, the French advocates of the Chicago approach were able to mount a major international conference, at the Université de Versailles Saint-Quentin-en-Yvelines, which brought together many of the surviving members of the post-war generation of Chicago PhD students (Allemand 1998). The event was attended by more than 350 French scholars – and a few from the UK!

Since 2000, French sociology has been buffeted by many of the economic gales that have affected higher education and research around the world. The faltering world economy has constrained budgets, or led to cuts, in ways that have limited the opportunities for new generations of researchers and university teachers to come through the system. Nevertheless, a number of significant shifts have occurred. French sociology has simultaneously become more diverse and more professional. The difficult environment has clearly encouraged sociologists to focus on what they share rather than on what divides them, as in the re-establishment of a professional association in 2002. Speaking in 2018, Stéphane Dufoix, a professor at Nanterre, which was at the center of May 1968, observes:

> Contemporary French sociology is particularly marked by the absence of "schools of thought". There is no dominant paradigm, no real conflict between two ways of investigating the social.
>
> *(Rousset 2018)*

Some traditional conflicts are not entirely resolved, as will be clear from Peneff's comments on some of the empiricist quantitative approaches that have, as in the UK, been promoted as the way forward for sociology. Nevertheless both quantitative and qualitative sociologists appear to have been able to agree on the importance of founding the discipline on empirical research rather than theoretical assumptions. Demazière's (2015) obituary for Dubar, for example, endorses the aspiration to "make sociology a recognized discipline, to emancipate it from social philosophy and superficial essays on fashionable topics,[14] to anchor it in empirical work and methodological requirements, and finally to secure a degree of autonomy and public recognition that remained fragile."

Although this book focusses on the influence of the Chicago tradition in US sociology, there has also been a wider engagement with other traditions like ethnomethodology and conversation analysis. Latour, for example, has effectively tried to "domesticate" these for French audiences by adopting a more "philosophical" style of writing. After twenty years on the margins, in a position at the *Ecole Nationale Supérieure des Mines*, which is principally an engineering school, he was appointed, in 2006, to a chair at *Sciences Po Paris*. This institution stands apart from the general French system of higher education as an internationally oriented, elite center for education and research in the social sciences. The chair at the *Collège de France* lay vacant for more than ten years but was filled by Pierre-Michel Menger from 2013. Menger's work applies economic sociology to the labor market for creative artists in ways that are much more empirically led than those of his predecessors. A third important figure would be Didier Fassin, working between anthropology and sociology, mainly in the fields of health and deviance, who has been based at Princeton since 2009 but continues to exercise significant influence in French academic circles. While French sociology retains a critical edge, it has become significantly less oppositional and more appreciative of the complexities of governing. However, as elsewhere, it has not been easy to translate this shift into substantial impacts on policy or practice. The contribution of sociology to a state apparatus that has moved toward New Public Management is ill-defined and uncertain (Berrebi-Hoffmann and Grémion 2009). This necessarily impacts on the resources that the state is willing to make available to the discipline. In summary, the current intellectual and material realities of French sociology are not nearly as different from those of the anglophone world as we might suppose from the selection of French scholars that we have chosen to recognize.

What's the Attraction of Howard Becker?

As I have already noted, Peneff is attracted by Becker's reluctance to engage in open conflicts with other scholars. By implication he is contrasting Becker's restraint with the practice of French academic life, which one commentator on a draft characterized as "*un sport de combat*" – we might translate this as "a blood sport." Reputations and careers are made through aggressive critiques rather than collaborative enterprises. France is not, of course, the only country where this happens, nor is sociology the only academic discipline with a high level of disputes. Becker's preference, as Peneff stresses throughout the book, is to lay out his own approach and to leave others to decide whether or not to adopt it. He welcomes people who approach him with a genuine interest but is not seeking disciples. This can be contrasted with the "master and apprentices" model that has dominated sociology in France, and of which Bourdieu was perhaps the last great exponent. Grémion (2005), for example, describes Bourdieu's creation of a journal, *Actes de la Recherche en Sciences Sociales*, of which he was sole editor, devoted to publishing the work of his followers:

> As to the modus operandi, one must see *Actes de la Recherche* less as a review with an editorial board than as the studio or atelier of a great academic painter. Just as apprentices are assigned different tasks in the painter's studio, sometimes even painting part of the canvas, in Bourdieu's atelier everyone worked toward the great fresco of society, alone or with the master on this or that field, before the master signed his name at the bottom of the canvas. From then on, Pierre Bourdieu composed his works using the output of his atelier.
>
> *(Grémion 2005, p. 9)*

More recently, Philippe Coulangeon has noted that:

> One of the features of Bourdieu's legacy is that he is the only one of the sociologists of his generation to have succeeded in creating a school of followers. There are, for example, very few social science researchers who would acknowledge the exclusive influence of Raymond Boudon.
>
> *(Rousset 2018)*

Since 1998, however, Becker (1998, 2007a, 2007b, 2017) has published a series of books that set out a position on method and methodology, rather than leaving his views to be inferred from accounts of his research. Peneff discusses the first three of these (*Tricks of the Trade, Telling about Society* and *Writing for Social Scientists*) and I shall introduce the most recent, *Evidence*, later in this section.

If we want to understand what Peneff is challenging, though, a convenient place to start is one of the rare occasions where Becker discusses another scholar's work, in a 2006 interview with Alain Pessin (2017). Pessin asks Becker to compare his idea of "world" with Bourdieu's concept of "field."

> Becker: The idea of world, as I think of it, is very different. Of course, it is still a metaphor. But the metaphor of world – which does not seem to be at all true of the metaphor of field – contains people, all sorts of people, who are in the middle of doing something which requires them to pay attention to each other, to take account consciously of the existence of others and to shape what they do in the light of what others do. In such a world, people do not respond automatically to mysterious external forces surrounding them. Instead, they develop their lines of activity gradually, seeing how others respond to what they do and adjusting what they do next in a way that meshes with what others have done and will probably do next...
>
> In contrast with the idea of "field," the idea of "world" seems to me more empirically grounded. It talks about things that we can observe – people doing things rather than "forces," "trajectories," "inertia," which are not observable in social life, if you understand these terms in the technical sense given to them in physics. We cannot observe these things perfectly, of course, but well enough that we can argue about them, and the procedures of empirical science can give us provisional answers of the kind science gives...
>
> Many social theories start with the premise that reality is hidden from ordinary mortals and that it takes a special competence, perhaps even a magical gift, to be able to see through these obstacles and discover The Truth. I have never believed that. To quote my mentor Hughes again, he often said that sociologists did not know anything that nobody knew. Whatever sociologists knew about social life, they had learned from someone who was part of and fully engaged in that area of life. But since, as Simmel had made clear in his essay on secrecy (Simmel 1950), knowledge is not equally distributed, everyone doesn't know everything. Not because people are blinded to reality by illusions, but because things have been kept from them by institutional arrangements (which may or may not have been put in place to achieve that end). Sociologists find out what this one knows and what that one knows so that, in the end, they can assemble the partial knowledge of participants into a more comprehensive understanding. The idea of "false consciousness" is a classic example of the theory of social knowledge opposed to my own practice.
>
> *(Becker and Pessin 2017, pp. 94, 103)*

Becker sets out here the fundamental difference between the induction characteristic of several generations of Chicago School sociologists and the deductive approaches more characteristic of the various schools of critical sociology. As Crozier noted in the earlier quote, Bourdieu presents critical sociology without the citations to Marx. His objective is *"dévoilement,"* unveiling The Truth to those who do not know it. It is an updating of the "false consciousness" that Becker rejects. I will return to this when I consider the conclusions Peneff draws for "public sociology." For the moment, though, I would like to focus on two key themes in this passage: that sociology is about studying people doing things, and that it is subject to "the procedures of empirical science [that] give provisional answers…"

Studying People Doing Things

Peneff illustrates Becker's commitment to "studying people doing things" through extensive discussions of the latter's work on art worlds (see also Pessin 2017). Traditionally, philosophers and art scholars have tried to find criteria for discriminating art as a special product of human culture and for ranking its products in terms of their approach to some aesthetic ideal. Art is thought of as a set of properties inherent in some object, although scholars differ on what these might be. Classically art is a representation of reality that somehow or other improves upon it. Art may reorganize reality so that it more closely approaches an ideal form, which is more symmetrical, harmonious, etc. Alternatively, art may go behind the surface appearances of reality to express some underlying essence. It finds the universal in the specific case. In particular, it is often thought to express an emotional or symbolic truth rather than a material or an intellectual one. Our experience of art both enriches us in a personal sense and deepens our understanding of the worlds of matter and spirit that we inhabit. Given the place of aesthetics within philosophy's heritage, and the cultural prestige of high art and those who write commentaries on it, we should not be surprised that it features prominently in Bourdieu's sociology of culture.

Bourdieu sought to move away from both the idea of unconscious structures of cognition in Lévi-Strauss and the version of Marxist thought developed by Louis Althusser and his followers, where individuals were simply bearers of the social structure. In recounting the history of the concepts of "habitus" and "field," he notes a desire to "put forward the 'creative', active and inventive capacities of habitus and of agent…" (Bourdieu 1985, p. 13). This, however, is somewhat at odds with his own formulation:

> The structures constitutive of a particular type of environment (e.g. the material conditions of existence characteristic of a class condition) produce *habitus*, systems of durable, transposable *dispositions*, structured structures predisposed to function as structuring structures, that is, as principles of the generation and structuring of practices and representations which can be objectively "regulated" and "regular" without in any way being the product of obedience to rules, objectively adapted to their goals without presupposing a conscious aiming at ends or an express mastery of the operations necessary to attain them and, being all this, collectively orchestrated without being the product of the orchestrating action of a conductor.
>
> *(Bourdieu 1977, p. 72)*

He goes on to state:

> Each agent, wittingly or unwittingly, willy nilly, is a producer and reproducer of objective meaning. Because his actions and works are the product of a *modus operandi* of which he is not the producer and has no conscious mastery, they contain an "objective intention" as the Scholastics put it, which always outruns his conscious intentions.
>
> *(Bourdieu 1977, p. 79)*

Let us first recall Crozier's observation that Bourdieu's work might be Marxist without the citations. Habitus is introduced through a classic rendition of material base and superstructure. Material conditions produce a stable set of dispositions that lead agents to act in particular ways. The agent is not a creative and conscious actor, nor is he or she a competent witness to their own intentions. The co-ordination of action is achieved by the internalization of the dispositions rather than by the agency of humans – there are no conductors of the orchestra. It is important not to go too far in criticism here: all sociologists recognize the role of the material world to a greater or lesser extent in shaping the possibilities for action. In this minimal sense, we are all Marxists. What is distinctive here is Bourdieu's positioning of the sociologist as someone who can objectively discover the dispositions and the relationships that they create between actors. From this, the sociological observer can come to char-acterize the habitus. By detaching the relationships and the dispositions from the actors, he sets up a position where the actors' knowledge and motivations are invi-sible and can only be revealed by the work of the sociologist. This stance lies squarely in the legacy of Durkheim:

> The suicide rate is…a factual order, unified and definite…these statistical data express the suicidal tendency with which each society is collectively afflicted… each society is predisposed to contribute a definite quota of voluntary deaths. This predisposition may therefore be the subject of a special study belonging to sociology.
>
> *(Durkheim 1952, p. 51)*

Bourdieu's innovation is to disaggregate Durkheim's societal "predisposition" and to see that different contexts within a society may each be bound together by a partial equivalent in the form of the habitus. These contexts are the "fields" that Becker discusses in his conversation with Pessin.

The concept of field is also an attempt to develop an alternative to the traditions of art criticism that stressed the autonomy of art as a domain and of the reductionist Marxism of earlier sociological writers like Lucien Goldmann:

> the most important group to which an individual may belong, from the point of intellectual and artistic activity and creation, is that of the social class, or classes of which he is a member…Each class will then express its desire for

change – or for permanence – by a complete vision both of what the man of the present day is, with his qualities and failings, and of what the man of the future ought to be...The men who express this vision on an imaginative or conceptual plane are writers and philosophers...

(Goldmann 1964, pp. 16–17)

Bourdieu (1985) credits the idea of a field to his reading of Max Weber's sociology of religion. Where Weber had described a set of interactions between agents, Bourdieu saw a structured set of relations that could provide a model or a template for the analysis of other spheres of human activity. To describe this, he adopts a vocabulary from economic theory, which he regards as another specific case of the general model:

The general theory of the economy of fields makes it possible to describe and to define the specific form taken by the most general mechanisms and concepts such as capital, investment, interest, within each field, and thus it allows one to avoid all kinds of reductionism, beginning with economism, which recognizes as valuable only material interest and the quest for the maximizing of monetary profit.

(Bourdieu 1985, p. 20)

By treating the language of economics metaphorically, Bourdieu is able to incorporate the symbolic and cultural aspects of the field, and the habitus that constitutes it for those within it: the notion of "cultural capital," for example, has been particularly influential.

Depending on the field in which it functions, and at the cost of the more or less expensive transformations which are the precondition for its efficacy in the field in question, capital can present itself in three fundamental guises: as *economic capital*, which is immediately and directly convertible into money and may be institutionalized in the forms of property rights; as *cultural capital*, which is convertible, on certain conditions, into economic capital and may be institutionalized in the forms of educational qualifications; and as *social capital*, made up of social obligations ("connections"), which is convertible, in certain conditions, into economic capital and may be institutionalized in the forms of a title of nobility.

(Bourdieu 1986, p. 243)

Having broadened the concept of capital, though, Bourdieu's approach to art does not make a fundamental break with either the classic traditions of aesthetics (hagiographic exaltation) or of Marxist writers on culture (reductive disparagement):

The researcher who seeks the principle of the existence of the work, what it has that is historic or transhistoric ...within the interests linked to the belonging to a field of cultural production, and, more broadly, to the social field in its totality, treats the work as an intentional sign associated with and regulated by some other thing, of which it is also a symptom. The researcher looks for the objective intention which is hidden beneath the declared intention. He supposes that a profound meaning, an expressive impulse, biological or social, is enunciated in it...In contrast to the angelic pure interest for pure form, the analysis which apprehends in one and the same motion the expressive impulse, the censure and the sublimation assured by the working into-form, offers a realistic view, that is to say, a truer and at the same time definitively a more reassuring view of the collective work of sublimation which is at the base of the greatest triumphs of human enterprise: history cannot produce the trans-historical universality except by producing, by means of often ruthless struggles of special interests, social universes which, through the effect of the social alchemy of their historical laws of functioning tend to extract from the confrontation of the special interests the sublimated essence of the universal. Hagiographic exaltation and reductive disparagement share the tendency to seek the source of great works in great men; and to overlook everything, in the most sublime practices and productions, which depends on the logic of these paradoxical universes where, among other reasons because they can reap profit from proving unselfishness certain men can find an incentive to surpass themselves or, at least, to produce actions or works which go beyond their intentions and their interests.

(*Bourdieu 1985, pp. 23–24*)

Bourdieu's "third way" transcends both the idea of the "angelic purity" of art works and the idea that they are mere expressions of class interest. It does not, however, depart from the notion that there is some layer of truth that can only be discovered by the sociological commentator. The work is a sign or a symbol that stands for some "profound meaning" beyond its "declared intention." The sociologist's analysis offers an account that is more realistic and more true than that of the actors involved because it recognizes and reaches into relations (alchemy) that are otherwise mysterious if not actually invisible. By describing the habitus, the relations of the field are unveiled. The actors are no more than the bearers of the habitus, the points at which the relations take on a material form.

As Pessin (2017) also notes, Becker's account of art worlds strips away most of the mysticism inherent in Bourdieu's approach: art is just a label that enough people apply to an artefact or an activity at some particular historical moment. The art world is made up of people who produce, buy and sell, and provide the material conditions within which these processes can occur. Looking back to his early experiences as a jazz musician in variously disreputable night clubs in Chicago, Becker recognizes that the cloakroom attendant at a gallery is as much a participant as the artist whose work is on sale or the critic who is evaluating it for a magazine or newspaper. Institutions are the aggregate outcome of people's work: "[T]he term 'an organization' is an abbreviation of the full term 'an organization of social actions'" (Garfinkel 1956, p. 181).

Why does Peneff prefer this approach? One part of the answer – his thinking about the relationship between sociology and society – will be discussed in the next section. His major thrust, though, is the way in which Becker stands for an approach that is empirical without being empiricist. An art world is to be discovered through the study of interactions rather than defined in advance and *ex cathedra* by a sociologist taking up a philosopher's agenda. Where Bourdieu (1964; 1979) presupposes the existence of cultural capital in studies like *Les Héritiers* or *La Distinction* as a basis for mapping relations of exclusion and inclusion, Becker sees this as a way of summarizing a set of conventions established by actors as devices for the co-ordination of their actions. This is not to deny the potential value of concepts like cultural or social capital so much as to say that they are to be inferred from the observation of actions and interactions rather than stipulated in advance. Cultural capital is a label that sociologists apply to a pattern of actions, and the shared understandings that generate them, rather than something that exists prior to the observations. At another level, to the extent that a term like "cultural capital" passes into sociological currency, then the invocation of the concept can itself become an object of study. Sociology is also people's work, carried out in organizational settings and shaped by the material and symbolic environments around it. There is a "sociological world" as much as an "art world" or the kinds of "hospital worlds" that Anselm Strauss and his collaborators wrote about.[15] The boundaries of a social world are set by the participants, not by the observer, although, of course, the participants may differ in where they draw these: the art critic may disregard the security personnel – but a strike of guards soon closes down a gallery.

Peneff also underlines Becker's acknowledgment of the role of chance and contingency in social life. Like most interactionists, Becker's approach is anti-teleological – there is no grand narrative, no underlying plan, no laws of social development. Interactionism rejects the utopian element that is present in most self-styled critical sociologies. We may be able to make modest progress in altering social conditions, although we should be wary of assuming that these will represent progress. Like ecologists, we can develop systematic accounts of the processes by which a particular order is achieved, in nature or in society, but that order is itself dynamic, homeostasis rather than equilibrium.[16] There is no end to history. Stuff just keeps on happening. We learn about society by becoming immersed in it – Peneff quotes an earlier Chicago sociologist, Robert Park, on the importance of first-hand observation. Sociology is not something to be done in a classroom or the seventeenth and eighteenth century buildings of the *Collège de France*.

The Procedures of Empirical Science

The second feature of Becker's approach that Peneff notes is his increasing insistence on the scientific nature of sociology. This is not science in the trivial sense that everything must be quantified – although Becker is more respectful of quantitative work than Peneff sometimes allows:

> Since all our knowledge is unsatisfactory and just a beginning, we shouldn't equate good science exclusively with the kind that uses numbers (or with its opposite) and should instead refuse to add to our troubles in making social science by engaging in that kind of intramural quarrelling. Nor should we equate good science exclusively with work whose warrant rests on long immersion in all the details of social interaction and its results as a way to understanding the organization of social life.
>
> *(Becker 2017, p. 22)*

Becker stresses the mutual respect between qualitative and quantitative traditions in the Chicago department and is concerned to restore this. Methods should be fitted to problems rather than being the subject of dogma. He challenges the advocates of each to look at the flaws and sources of error in their own practices – and to consider how these might be repaired – rather than to engage in periodic rounds of denunciation and hostility.

Becker consolidates much of his thinking about method in *Evidence*, published in 2017 and too late for Peneff to include in the original text of this book. *Evidence* explores the relationship between *ideas, data*, and *evidence*, which Becker sees as the three phases of any scientific enterprise. They create a circle of interdependencies that we can join at any point: data may become evidence to check out ideas or data may generate ideas we seek to test by assembling evidence. *Data* are the recorded traces of observations – field notes, survey forms, official documents, social media links, etc. – from which researchers make science. These data become *evidence* when they are used to support an argument, using criteria that establish data as valid representations of the observed events from which inferences can be made about an *idea*, or system of ideas – a "theory." Becker follows a distinction recognized by mathematicians between a "proof" that is achieved by demonstrative reasoning, codified in the rules of formal logic, and a "conjecture," which is supported by "plausible" reasoning. All knowledge that is not a mathematical proof is conjecture, as supported by whatever counts as plausible reasoning in a particular social world. As such, it is necessarily provisional, contestable and open to revision in the light of new data or changing criteria of evidence. The actors within social worlds create processes that establish what is to be considered "true for all practical purposes."[17] Much of the book is then devoted to examining the conventions used by sociologists to evaluate the transformation of data into evidence and the assessment of their plausibility.

Following the work of Alain Desrosières (1993), Becker sets up two models of scientific process that were articulated by the eighteenth-century scientists, Linnaeus and Buffon.

> Linnaeus defined the job as slotting research results into the proper boxes in the scheme he had constructed. Buffon saw it as continuing to create new boxes as new facts came to light
>
> *(Becker 2017, p. 24)*

Becker recalls a story that he heard, as a graduate student, from Robert Redfield (1897–1958), an eminent anthropologist and contemporary of Everett Hughes, about a former dean in the 1930s who had the habit of asking faculty members: "What brick have you added to the wall of social science this week?" Becker sees this as marking the classic research designs of quantitative social science research, where a literature review defines a problem space that can be investigated by a planned inquiry. He contrasts this with the iterative processes of discovery that have marked his own research, where bricks and foundations emerge from the continuing investigation. This only terminates at a point where time, money or enthusiasm run out. This stance is very characteristic of his generation of researchers. It must be remembered that, as recently as the 1960s, there was a very limited body of qualitative social science research studies. This is partly why Barney Glaser and Anselm Strauss (1967) put so much emphasis on discovery in *The Discovery of Grounded Theory*, a position that Glaser maintained and Strauss did not. Strauss eventually came to a position that allowed a bigger role for theory-building in a Linnaean fashion as more studies were completed. We could use other research reports to sketch the shape of walls, identify holes and select potential sites where we could look for bricks to fill them. As Becker (2007a, 2014) explains elsewhere, his own approach rests very much on the comparison of cases, seeking to identify the elements that make them similar or different and creating taxonomies. While this may be in the spirit of Buffon, it does not prevent other qualitative researchers from adopting a more Linnaean approach.[18]

Whether you are a follower of Linnaeus or of Buffon, Becker emphasizes the probabilistic nature of social science knowledge. He quotes Stanley Lieberson, who is best known as a quantitative methodologist, with approval:

> in a complex multivariate world, it is unrealistic to act as if social life is driven by deterministic forces, even if we think that it is. Since there is such a wide array of conditions affecting an outcome, it is naïve to think that a correct theory will predict or even explain the outcome in any given circumstance. Only the most simplistic and mechanical conception would assume that a theory has to be the dominant influence in all historical settings and contexts, regardless of the heterogeneity of the units.
>
> *(Lieberson 1992, p. 7)*

In this discussion, we can see more of the features that attract Peneff in his critique of Bourdieu. Where Grémion (2005) sees Bourdieu's apprentices filling out the Linnaean fields that he has constructed, and Becker (2017) himself identifies Bourdieu's "deterministic forces" in his use of metaphors from physics, Peneff is seeing the possibility of creating a more open kind of sociological inquiry, more modest in its goals but truer to the situations and events being studied. A probabilistic social science is still worth having: UK cycling came to dominate its sport by a focus on "marginal gains." Shifting the odds of achieving a desired outcome by 2 percent or 5 percent is still worth doing and may be more effective than waiting for a revolutionary moment of disruption.

This is absolutely not to imply that "anything goes" in qualitative social science research. This is a recurrent theme in Becker's late work. He underlines the importance of being clear precisely what an investigator has done – for this reason he would actually like to junk the term "ethnography" for its vagueness. Data from direct observation does not have the same status as data from interviews at one remove from the events. They are different kinds of evidence that point to different things (see also Dingwall 1997). Researchers need to be clear about the boundary conditions around their findings: all hospitals cannot be assumed to be the same, nor can all ghettoes. We need to establish clarity in defining our cases and consider what might constitute significant sources of variation. My own study of child protection decision-making (Dingwall et al. 1983) offers an example. The main research site was a relatively affluent English county. As a team, however, we deliberately chose to undertake comparative fieldwork in a poorer and more remote rural county and in part of a "rustbelt" metropolitan area. (If we had had more time and funding, we would also have looked at an ethnically mixed inner city neighborhood.) To the extent that our findings in each area were similar, we felt confident that our generalizations were characteristic of child protection in England as a whole. At the same time, we also found features that were specific to each site and were able to assess how the particular details of local history, geography, and the enthusiasms of particular professionals had created variations on these themes. A single legal and agency framework was open to a considerable, but not indefinite, range of interpretations and practices.

Becker urges a systematic concern for possible sources of error, for the checking of subjective reports, where appropriate, and for the consideration of deviant cases and negative evidence. A major flaw with many current studies in his view, is the researcher's desire to sustain conclusions that they knew in advance. Again, we can see what attracts Peneff, in the repudiation of the prior anti-establishment position, also identified by Crozier. Qualitative research is not a question of seeking to illustrate what any righteous person takes for granted. It is about inquiry, investigation, and challenge – to orthodoxies of the left as much as of the right.

Pessin's interview with Becker concludes by restating the essential contrasts between the approach that he takes, advocated by Peneff, and that of Bourdieu and his followers:

> Pessin: A sociology of situations as opposed to a sociology of structures, process versus habitus, career versus disposition, openness versus closure, choice versus determination – the exercise of analysis we have gone through, it seems to me, shows very clearly that the idea of world is in no way a "soft version" of the theory of field. One could, moreover, add that it proceeds from observation, and is very suspicious of theory. These are not two differently nuanced versions of an approach which essentially refer to the same thing. They are two ways of thinking which are opposed in their intentions and, necessarily, in

their results: the philosophico-sociological approach which searches for the essence of the social, which leads to the theory of fields, and the sociologico-ethnographic approach which tries to make explicit the circumstances in which social situations create links between actors, the idea of world.

Becker: You have captured here all the essential differences between the approaches: the one open to multiple possibilities, discovered in the course of immersion in social life; the other focused on demonstrating, on the basis of a priori considerations, the truth of an already established abstract philosophical position. I have nothing to add.

(Becker and Pessin 2017, p. 104)

Peneff argues that we should opt for "multiple possibilities" rather than "previously established truths."

Sociology and the Public

Where does this leave the relationship between sociology and society? Recall Becker's words in the interview with Pessin, quoted earlier:

Many social theories start with the premise that reality is hidden from ordinary mortals and that it takes a special competence, perhaps even a magical gift, to be able to see through these obstacles and discover The Truth. I have never believed that. To quote my mentor Hughes again, he often said that sociologists did not know anything that nobody knew. Whatever sociologists knew about social life, they had learned from someone who was part of and fully engaged in that area of life. But since, as Simmel had made clear in his essay on secrecy (Simmel 1950), knowledge is not equally distributed, everyone doesn't know everything., Not because people are blinded to reality by illusions, but because things have been kept from them by institutional arrangements (which may or may not have been put in place to achieve that end). Sociologists find out what this one knows and what that one knows so that, in the end, they can assemble the partial knowledge of participants into a more comprehensive understanding. The idea of "false consciousness" is a classic example of the theory of social knowledge opposed to my own practice.

(Becker and Pessin 2017, p. 103)

Peneff uses Becker to oppose Bourdieu's notions of *dévoilement* or unveiling and his efforts through the columns of *Le Monde* to use sociology as a vehicle for an overt critique of French society and politics. For Becker, it is hard enough to understand the empirical world of here and now, and the historical events that have shaped it. Peneff emphasizes Becker's reluctance to prescribe actions on the basis of his research. Actions are for citizens to determine – sociology is a means to better inform them about options, choices, and consequences, the "multiple possibilities" to which Becker alludes. Professional humility is a recurrent theme of Peneff's account. We should not tell others how to live, we should not seek power and patronage in our workplaces, we should not claim expertise that we do not possess.

In this opposition, Peneff is constructing a template for a much wider debate. Bourdieu has been claimed as a model by the movement for public sociology (Burawoy 2014, pp. 388–389), which often caricatures its critics as sell-outs or careerists. Peneff suggests that Becker offers an alternative model that is less utopian, more democratic and more respectful of diversity. It is important to stress that this is not a recipe for disengagement but for engagement on different terms. It is a positive alternative to the "professional sociology" depicted by Burawoy:

> The original passion for social justice, economic equality, human rights, sustainable environment, political freedom or simply a better world, that drew so many of us to sociology, is channeled into the pursuit of academic credentials. Progress becomes a battery of disciplinary techniques – standardized courses, validated reading lists, bureaucratic rankings, intensive examinations, literature reviews, tailored dissertations, refereed publications, the all-mighty CV, the job search, the tenure file, and then policing one's colleagues and successors to make sure we all march in step. Still, despite the normalizing pressures of careers, the originating moral impetus is rarely vanquished, the sociological spirit cannot be extinguished so easily...we are more than ready to embark on a systematic back-translation, taking knowledge back to those from whom it came, making public issues out of private troubles, and thus regenerating sociology's moral fiber. Herein lies the promise and challenge of public sociology, the complement and not the negation of professional sociology.
>
> *(Burawoy 2005a, p. 5)*

Although Burawoy is at some pains to concede the value of professional sociology, this is primarily as an institutional base for public sociology. He paraphrases Marx: "If our predecessors set out to change the world we have too often ended up conserving it" (Burawoy 2005, p. 5).[19] He sets out a vision, strongly influenced by the Italian Marxist, Antonio Gramsci (1891–1937), of *organic public sociology* [20] in which:

> As mirror and conscience of society, sociology must define, promote and inform public debate about deepening class and racial inequalities, new gender regimes, environmental degradation, market fundamentalism, state and non-state violence.
>
> *(Burawoy 2002)*

> The sociologist works in close connection with a visible, thick, active, local and often counter-public...a labor movement, neighborhood associations, communities of faith, immigrant rights groups, human rights organizations.
>
> *(Burawoy 2005a, p. 7)*

We might say that critical engagement with real utopias is today an integral part of the project of sociological socialism. It is a vision of socialism that places human society, or social humanity at its organizing center, a vision that was central to Marx but that was too often lost before it was again picked up by Gramsci and Polanyi. If public sociology is to have a progressive impact it will have to hold itself continuously accountable to some such vision of democratic socialism.

(Burawoy 2005b, p. 325)

Burawoy speaks for many contemporary sociologists in this vision, and in his construction of a particular historical narrative for sociology. This selectively reads the traditional canon and adds figures representative of present-day minorities and excluded groups. It reads yesterday very much in terms of today.

Peneff's account of Becker takes us in a different direction. Becker is very reluctant to set up himself as a moralist or a utopian. While he makes no particular secret of his own liberal and humane values, he is reluctant to impose them on anyone else. To some extent, this is a voice of experience: one of the interesting revelations in *Evidence* is his admission that his original work on moral entrepreneurs, using the case of Harry Anslinger, Director of the US Federal Narcotics Bureau, was completely mistaken (Becker 2017, pp. 191–192). Anslinger was not a "Puritan nut" but a rational actor in efforts to regulate the market in legal narcotics in order to protect the pharmaceutical industry. The concept may still have value, but the data were not there to support the original statement. To some extent it is about his fundamental awareness of the provisional and uncertain status of all knowledge. Human interaction generates very complex systems and interventions are not necessarily guaranteed to produce predictable results. In other contexts, we take this for granted – Becker regularly refers to the work of Diane Vaughan (e.g. 1997), for example, who is one of the leading analysts of organizational failures. Why would we think that social systems at a societal level were less complex than those at an institutional or organizational level?

In this respect, Becker sits more comfortably within a mainstream sociological tradition. Although both Durkheim and Weber described themselves as socialists or social democrats, neither envisaged the sort of revolutionary transformation that Marx depicted. Both were much more focused on pragmatic reforms to improve the efficiency, effectiveness, equity, and civility of capitalist societies. The Chicago tradition was no more radical – Albion Small and Charles Vincent concluded their 1894 textbook with these words:

We have attempted to make students suspicious of all apparently easy solutions to the problems of society… we once more propose the scholarly ideal – *not investigation as a substitute for civic service but investigation as both promise and performance of civic duty*…Scientific students of society ought to oppose with all their power the many mischievous tendencies to construct mountainous social philosophies out of molehills of social knowledge… This is not to urge that sociologists should be reactionaries. There is little likelihood that men who personally observe actual social conditions, according to the method which we propose, instead of speculating about them in the study, will want to fold their hands and let social evil work out its own salvation. In the interest of larger and truer knowledge, and better social cooperation in the future, it is, nevertheless, necessary to distinguish very clearly between provisional action prompted by sympathy, and the discovery of social principles attested by science.

(Small and Vincent 1894, pp. 373–374)

In many ways, this is closer to the conservative political philosophy of a writer like Michael Oakeshott.

To be conservative, then, is to prefer the familiar to the unknown, to prefer the tried to the untried, fact to mystery, the actual to the possible, the limited to the unbounded, the near to the distant, the sufficient to the superabundant, the convenient to the perfect, present laughter to utopian bliss.

(Oakeshott 1991, p. 407)

It also echoes Karl Popper's notion of "piecemeal social engineering":

The piecemeal engineer knows…how little he knows. He knows that we can learn only from our mistakes. Accordingly, he will make his way, step by step, carefully comparing the results expected with the results achieved and always on the look-out for the unavoidable unwanted consequences of any reform; and he will avoid undertaking reforms of a complexity and scope which make it impossible for him to disentangle causes and effects, and to know what he is really doing…Holistic or Utopian social engineering.. is never of a "private" but always of a "public" character. It aims at remodeling the "whole of society" in accordance with a definite plan or blueprint…

(Popper 1961, p. 67)

This version of conservatism, it should be stressed is neither reactionary, nor populist, nor neo-liberal, nor any of the other slogans that have been used in recent years. It accepts the need for social, economic, and technological change but urges caution and skepticism about their direction and potential benefits. Although it has a certain tendency toward individualism, this is in the interests of understanding a social world as a whole, giving equal attention to all the participants – as I have described this elsewhere, to "top dogs, bottom dogs and, indeed, lap dogs, and their respective contributions to the observable character of some organised social action" (Dingwall, 1980, p. 874). This can easily be mischaracterized as indifference or inertia, if the metric is column inches in *Le Monde*. It is rather, as Becker suggests in his interview with Pessin, a concern to "assemble the partial knowledge of participants into a more comprehensive understanding" as a basis for social actions or interventions. Sociologists should not be aiming to replace Shelley's poets as the legislators of the world.[21]

Running through Peneff's account is a stress on the humility of the sociologist. In the French context, this is understandable. Power has often been sought for personal gain or in pursuit of political agendas, much as Burawoy sees the university as a material base for adventures in public sociology. Peneff praises Becker's refusal to seek preferment or office in favor of a focus on a life of scholarship. It is an emphasis on the vocational aspects of sociology, of sociology as a calling in the Weberian sense. This is an important debate to be had. Maybe anyone who actively wants to be a department chair or a dean should be disqualified by virtue of that desire? On the other hand, sociology, like any other scientific enterprise rests on a material base. The supply of resources needs to be secured, which involves work to sustain the legitimacy of the discipline in the eyes of those who pay for it. Teaching needs to be organized, employers need to be told about the value of sociology graduates, and those of our community who are not justifying their academic salaries need to be encouraged to consider their futures.

> ...sociology has always been suspicious of a worldly concern for efficiency and effectiveness, the stock in trade of the manager or policy maker. In this it shares the British academic disdain for the homme d'affaires. If you look up the word "management" in Raymond Williams's book, *Keywords* (1976: 156–8), for instance, his main concern seems to be that it derives from an old Italian term for training horses. In true romantic fashion, Williams manages to imply that this might be just about acceptable for the beasts but certainly not for human beings. The sociological literature on the National Health Service, to give an example nearer to home, almost invariably uses "managerialism" as a term of abuse. It is only acceptable to be on the side of the sick and under-privileged...But a Stoic social science would recognize that this denies the common humanity of managers who see their task precisely as providing better care.
>
> *(Strong and Dingwall 1989, p. 65)*

Qualitative sociologists can be effective academic managers, particularly as they understand how to work with people rather than metrics. The disciplines of field research with its emphasis on building relationships with a diverse range of people, of reflecting critically on language and social interaction, of understanding the importance of symbolism and culture as much as economics, are all important to successful leadership. Above all, the ethical sensibilities cultivated in field research shape the sense of responsibility required by anyone who has some degree of power over others: actions are not about personal gain or vanity but about the interests of a collectivity – a team, a workgroup, or a discipline (Dingwall and McDonnell 2015). Peneff's praise for Becker's acknowledgment of his own interests – and possibly his limitations – may need to be tempered by a recognition that this act of refusal may be less of a model than the reasoning that has led to it. It is, perhaps, more a question of why we might want to take on a leadership role, and the sensibility that we would bring to it, than a flat rejection of such roles per se. Great leaders are the servants of those whom they lead: the led are not there to flatter the leader.

Conclusion

Jean Peneff repeatedly emphasizes the way in which Howard Becker's understanding of jazz is also that of his approach to sociology. Much contemporary sociology can be compared with classical traditions in music, where players act out a script, with only a limited space for individual variations, which leads toward a resolution that has been ordained from the start. Jazz, on the other hand, is about improvisation, where real men and women use their human skills to create order in the here and now. The result is not anarchy because it rests on human capacities and conventions that provide initial forms and structures which can be remodeled in the moment. It is, however, anti-utopian in that there is no ultimate direction or destination. The performance comes to an agreed conclusion for the time being: the outcome will not necessarily be the same on the next occasion this particular blues is performed, even if by the same ensemble. The goal for sociology is not to impose a particular vision of a "better" world but to facilitate the process of improvisation so that ordinary men and women can shape their own destinies in a more informed way.

A Note on the Translation

Both the original author and commissioning editor have encouraged me to produce a fairly free translation of the original text. The grammatical structures of the French language, for example, allow sentences and paragraphs to be longer and more complex than English readers are comfortable with. Since one of Jean Peneff's rallying calls is for sociologists to adopt the simple and direct style of writing that Howard Becker advocates, it would be perverse to reproduce his French so accurately that it became obscure in English. My objective then has been to aim to produce the text that Peneff might have produced if it had originally been written in English, even if this involves breaking up sentences or splitting paragraphs. One feature that I have retained, though, is the use of the literary device of apostrophe, which often takes the form of invented quotes attributed to Howard Becker in order to represent his views. This is more common in French than in English. Where a quote can be sourced, it has been. The translation omits some pages of the original bibliography where Peneff discusses and lists the French translations of Becker's work. If these are directly cited in the text, they appear in the present bibliography. Where a work is cited in French in the references, any direct quotes are also my own translation. Where there is an existing English translation, this has been cited alongside details of the French original and substituted for Peneff's French version. All the endnotes are mine.

Acknowledgments

My first thanks go to Jean Peneff and Howard Becker for the support, encouragement, and constructive advice that they have provided throughout a project that has taken rather longer than any of us hoped. I would also like to acknowledge the vision and entrepreneurial flair of Mitch Allen, who originally commissioned the book and negotiated the translation rights. Katherin Ong and Marc Stratton, for Routledge, have been most patient in the delays that have dogged the actual delivery. I have learned a great deal about French higher education and social science over many years from Emilie Cloatre, Emmanuel Lazega, and Carine Vassy. Emmanuel and Carine both gave me invaluable feedback on the first draft of the introduction to this book and Emilie taught me most of what I know about the work of Bruno Latour. I am also grateful to my wife, Pam Watson, who is always the sharpest critic of my stylistic excesses. Marie Selwood has applied her professional skills in creating the index. None of them of course is any way responsible for what I have done with their advice.

This book is also something of a tribute to two inspiring French teachers, Scott Cooper and Arthur Craven, who understood that there was more to learning a language than vocabulary and grammar. They saw that a language was also a window onto another society, another culture and another way of looking at the world. In many ways their classes were the beginnings of my education as a sociologist, in understanding that the experience of Imperial Britain was not a foundation of Truth, Morality, and Justice by which the rest of the planet should be judged.

Notes

1 I use anglophone throughout this introduction as a shorthand for the whole global community of sociologists working primarily in English. While the largest groups are in the USA, Canada, Australia, and the United Kingdom, many other national sociologies know international work mainly through what gets published in English to serve one or more of these markets.

2 The descriptions of contemporaries (Fournier 2013, pp. 719–723) are certainly consistent with a severe depression, but could also indicate heart failure or some types of cancer.

3 The Dreyfus Affair was a political scandal that engulfed France from 1894 to 1906. Captain Alfred Dreyfus was a French army officer of Jewish descent who was convicted of passing secret papers to Germany. Although evidence rapidly appeared to show that he had been framed, the military establishment sought to maintain a cover-up. The affair raised many issues, including the place of anti-semitism in French national culture. In response, many Jewish politicians and intellectuals, whether secularized or actively practicing their faith, felt obliged to put on overt demonstrations of their patriotism.

4 More recent work suggests that Chapoulie's verdict may have been a little harsh, underestimating the degree of "culture shock" experienced by Halbwachs in his encounter with the vibrant city of Chicago (Halbwachs 2012; see also Becker 2012).

5 Alain Touraine (1977, p. 67) wrote: "When I used to go to see those great men of the universities or the CNRS, who happened to be communists, they did not hide from me their distrust of sociology, a bourgeois science. We were crushed between the thinking of the Communist Party, which rejected every study of society, which imposed dogmas that were flatly contradicted by reality – like that of the tendency to absolute

pauperization – and a wave of reactionary, transatlantic thought, which was imported by a decaying socialist party."

6 In France, higher level teaching and research are supported through two different institutional systems, with many established scholars and scientists having paid positions or honorary affiliations in both at the same time. Research is mostly carried out through the Centre National de la Recherche Scientifique (CNRS) which sustains research groups in all academic disciplines. Teaching is mostly carried out in universities, at least at an undergraduate level – PhD training is more usually located in CNRS groups. There are full-time postdoctoral positions with CNRS and a number of more senior full-time posts, equivalent to professorial appointments. In general, CNRS work is better paid and more prestigious than university work.

7 From the spring of 1968 through to the summer of 1969, most developed countries in Europe and North America experienced a period of social unrest in which university students played a prominent role. The turbulence took different forms in different countries around different grievances. Most took some inspiration from the US struggles of the 1960s over Civil Rights for people of color and the Vietnam War. To this were added particular institutional grievances around university structures that were poorly designed for the mass education of students who were legally adults. There were also economic grievances about the limited ability of the labor market in some countries to absorb the graduates produced by mass higher education. Actions were legitimized by reference to a loose political ideology that became known as the New Left. While this drew on some Marxist traditions, particularly as developed by the Frankfurt School, it was also informed by critics of colonialism, like Franz Fanon. A number of young sociologists were prominent in developing this body of work. In France, students were, for a short time, able to forge alliances with discontented industrial workers to the point of threatening the stability of the state. However, the French Communist Party negotiated an economic settlement of the workers' issues that allowed the conservative government to suppress the student movement with considerable brutality.

8 The Collège is a uniquely French institution, founded in 1530. There are currently fifty-two full professors, who are expected to spend most of their time on research and intellectual leadership, with modest teaching obligations. These are the most prestigious appointments available to a scholar in France.

9 My own sources suggest that Touraine was not in good health at the time and may have lacked energy rather than motivation.

10 Although not linked with Bourdieu, the controversy over the "self-promotion" of certain candidates in 2009 is a good example. In France matters concerning the qualification of individuals for appointment to university positions, tenure and promotion are handled centrally by the *Conseil National des Universités* through approximately eighty discipline-based committees. Two-thirds of the members are elected by established university teachers and one-third are nominated by the ministry of education. In 2009, the ministry nominations created a voting bloc of post-modernists on the committee covering sociology and demography, who proceeded to award promotions to their own members, despite conventions that this should be a rare event. (Some of those involved had also been participants in the equally contentious "Affaire Tessier" in 1999, where an astrologer had been awarded a PhD from the Sorbonne for a post-modernist thesis defending her work as science.) This resulted in widespread criticism from the profession, mass resignations of elected members, and a crisis of confidence that has yet to be fully resolved (Histoires d Universités 2009).

11 A former graduate student in Crozier's research group observes that he was never heard to criticize Bourdieu in that context. However, this is an interview three years after Bourdieu's death where Crozier is clearly trying to place a number of his views – on this and other subjects – into the public record.

12 This raises questions that cannot be pursued here about whether Goffman is to be read as more concerned with structures or with agency. Clearly, there are structuralist readings of his work in this period – see the discussion by Gonos (1977) – although his later

work, especially "Felicity's Condition" (Goffman 1983) places more emphasis on agency.

13 It should also be noted that there are significant legal barriers in France to maintaining official statistics or asking questions in publicly funded surveys about race or ethnicity (INSEE 2016). However, it is possible to support ethnographic studies of neighborhoods that just happen to have a high density of residents from a particular racial or ethnic group…

14 This echoes Crozier's comments on Bourdieu's association with the leading French newspaper, *Le Monde*.

15 A bibliography of Strauss's writings on social worlds can be found at http://dne2.ucsf. edu/public/anselmstrauss/pdf/work-socworlds_bib.pdf [accessed January 15, 2018].

16 On the ecological aspects of Chicago sociology, see Dingwall (2016). *Homeostasis* is a term from biology which describes the attempt of a system to return to a particular state in an environment that is constantly changing. It is different from *equilibrium*, which assumes that there is a stable state to which the system will return if disrupted. A common example of homeostasis would be central heating or air conditioning, where the system is constantly making minor adjustments in response to changing weather conditions or user movements to maintain a target temperature within a building.

17 This may include delegation to some other group of specialists. I have argued elsewhere, for example, that much of the work of professions rests on their role as managers of uncertainty. Civil courts resolve the unavoidable ambiguities of language by producing authoritative and uncontestable declarations of what documents like contracts, title deeds, conveyances or wills really mean. Their decisions can be taken as matters of fact that end arguments, at least for immediate purposes, and allow everyday life to move on (Dingwall 1999).

18 I had never heard Redfield's story until I read *Evidence*. Curiously, however, as my own PhD students will testify, I have used exactly the same phrase with many of them in seeking to construct qualitative research projects that were manageable within the time and resources available to a UK graduate student. This never eliminated the possibility of discovery but it focused their questions and choices of research site around foreshadowed problems rather than expecting them to work these out anew.

19 The *Eleventh Thesis on Feuerbach*, originally written in 1845: "The philosophers have only *interpreted* the world, in various ways; the point, however, is to *change* it" (Marx and Engels 1968, p. 30; original italics).

20 Gramsci is often cited as an inspiration for the notion of an "organic working class intellectual," who comes from and is aligned with labor movements – and, by extension, to similar individuals and social positioning in relation to other movements associated with historically or currently excluded groups. His original discussion in *Prison Notebooks* (Hoare and Nowell Smith 1971, pp. 131–162) is more concerned with the distinction between the "traditional" intellectuals of feudal or pre-modern societies and the "organic" intellectuals who emerge within all classes in the course of modernization. The latter elaborate the culture, technology, and ideological legitimations of each new class as it emerges.

21 "It is impossible to read the compositions of the most celebrated writers of the present day without being startled with the electric life which burns within their words. They measure the circumference and sound the depths of human nature with a comprehensive and all-penetrating spirit, and they are themselves perhaps the most sincerely astonished at its manifestations; for it is less their spirit than the spirit of the age. Poets are the hierophants of an unapprehended inspiration; the mirrors of the gigantic shadows which futurity casts upon the present; the words which express what they understand not; the trumpets which sing to battle and feel not what they inspire; the influence which is moved not, but moves. Poets are the unacknowledged legislators of the world" (Shelley 1840, pp. 56–57).

PREFACE TO THE FRENCH EDITION

How can we describe Howard Becker's work to people who are not familiar with it? How can we set out the common themes in his writings to those who have only read a few of them? Some of his books have not been translated into French. He has published many articles and notes in a wide variety of journals and reviews. These are, however, exactly the reasons why we should try to bring together the thinking of this most French of American sociologists. All of this is set within the framework of the famous Chicago School, which is the source of Becker's original contributions to sociology.

I have, though, long been uncertain about how best to approach this task. There are several versions of the "French Becker," as indicated by the sales figures for his books, their numerous reissues and new editions, and the well-established, and continuing, interest in his analyses and studies. If I cannot be certain about what is best, I have at least tried to be consistent, by locating Becker's work within the classical sociological canon and by identifying his original contribution: in insisting, for example, on the way chance and indeterminacy shape the historical and bio-graphical context of any sociological analysis. In this way, we can understand how he came to introduce radical innovations which, separated from the weight of detail in any particular case, may seem trivial or banal. As these pages unfold, we shall also meet Everett Hughes, Eliot Freidson, and Erving Goffman – his equals as innovators – and discover the recipes, tips, and tricks that Becker offers to other researchers. In reading Becker, we will explore the craft of writing sociology in clear and simple language, which has been his goal throughout his scholarly career. We will ask how he has remained inventive, original, and incisive for so long. It is not easy to continue to develop new thinking when one has discovered such a rich seam of ideas. One of his own chapters carries the title "Standardization and Innovation" (Becker 2007a, pp. 71–91): what balance between these is any society prepared to accept?

For all these reasons, I would place Becker alongside innovative historians, anthropologists, and scientists like Jack Goody, Richard Evans, John Dunn, Jean-Marc Lévy-Leblond, Jean-Clément Martin, and Karl Pomeranz. All of them have shaken up our conventional thinking through their provocative books. With one imaginative leap, they take us away from well-trodden paths to places where we can breathe a fresh kind of air. If we read them together with Becker's work, as I have had the opportunity to do since the 1980s, we can see that they are boldly pushing us toward an intellectual revolution. Their analyses have transformed our understanding of the history of the West. Their approach is so different from what currently passes for conventional European thought that they have shocked many readers. Becker (2007a) has played a key part in this, thanks to his stunning book, *Telling about Society*. Indeed! How can we talk about society – right here and right now?

INTRODUCTION TO THE FRENCH EDITION

The man who is the subject of this book is probably the best-known, and most widely published, living sociologist. His work has been translated in many countries: Argentina, Brazil, Japan, Korea, Italy, Portugal, Sweden and, most recently, Croatia. The reasons for his success, however, remain obscure. Although widely praised, his work has been entirely ignored in other countries, particularly in the German-speaking world. Their neglect of this highly regarded writer gives us an uneven and eccentric map of his impact. We might say that such disparities are both common and natural in a discipline like sociology whose boundaries are fluid and loosely defined. Indeed, we are a young discipline – little more than one hundred years old – which has not been universally adopted and whose legitimacy remains contested. Becker's books, though, also escape traditional intellectual categorizations. The fragments of his biography that he lets slip here and there in interviews are purely professional – he says little about his private life. They insist on the random character of all careers: he explains his own as a matter of chance, an unexpected opportunity to replace a professor at Chicago who had been injured in a streetcar accident.

What is it about this man that provokes such differing responses, that sees him as a source of light or casts him into the shadows? Certainly, like Bourdieu, he is an author known around the world, as indicated by the many translations of his writings. At the same time his work has generated little in the way of commentary and discussion. Is he a reformer? A rebel? A cool iconoclast? An anti-theoretical dilettante? All of these descriptions have been applied to him but none of them exactly fit. An American author who loves France to the point of living there for several months each year cannot, though, be a person to be taken lightly.

Becker is not the favorite author of any particular editor – six different people have worked on ten or so translations into French. He has neither received subsidies for the publication of his books, nor attracted the support of any particular intellectual faction or set of followers. We can, then, see him as someone who is unclassifiable, who does not display any of the fashionable characteristics of prestigious thinkers. Becker is a scholar who has quietly gone his own way for the last sixty years. He may not seem to qualify to join the ranks of the truly great, the immortals of our discipline. He does not fit the criteria for glory set by our media because his publications and his style are far outside the traditional models of academic sociology. They cannot be fitted into any particular specialty which he has claimed as his own. This does not bother him. Some have hailed his work as a breakthrough, but nothing seems to explain it: not his own background; not his sociological education at the University of Chicago, which was both classical and atypical; not some kind of inheritance – there are no great scholars among his ancestors. In brief, he constitutes, in his own life, a challenge to the theory of cultural capital and its transmission that would attempt to explain his rise through the cumulative interaction of various factors. Moreover, except in teaching and examining, he does not like to exercise the hierarchical power of his position. He consistently rejects the use of authority to promote his scholarly work. In his own unique way, Becker places himself on the margins of the institutionalized university, one foot inside and one outside.

His story has a further strange twist when we realize that he is also a professional musician. The compositions that he plays are not part of the classical canon analyzed by Max Weber, the great theorist and lover of music, although Becker admires his study, *The Rational and Social Foundations of Music* (Weber 1958). Becker is not the enlightened amateur or the frustrated virtuoso that we sometimes find among sociologists from wealthy backgrounds. He made a living as a backing pianist in night clubs. He was one of the innumerable jazz musicians playing in Chicago at the end of World War II in the bars and strip joints favored by businessmen on a binge or servicemen on leave. What an affront to the dignity of the world of learning in general, and to the moral earnestness of sociology in particular!

Becker continued to play in public until quite recently – for his own pleasure, for student society events or for academics at their conferences. Together with three or four associates, he would improvise a jam session on one evening of the American Sociological Association annual meetings in order to cheer up his serious colleagues after their labors of the day. Why would a renowned intellectual amuse himself in this fashion? If it were only childishness, it might be overlooked. However, Becker consistently brings his two crafts into confrontation, seeing them both as resources for developing the skills of observation. He has illustrated this in a book with one of his colleagues, Robert R. Faulkner, also a sociologist and a musician, in this case a trumpet player (Faulkner and Becker 2009). The book unites their shared passions for sociology and jazz. Starting from their experiences as musicians, combining participant observation with interviews, they have studied the practice of professional jazz players, the evolution of their trade, the interaction between generations, and the forms of apprenticeship.

What other role can music play in the world of scholarship? Can art and science live happily together, as the physicist Jean-Marc Lévy-Leblond (2010) has asked? Is it possible to conceive of a musical style within sociological writing? There is only one other example of a distinguished writer who was also a professional musician earning a living from his skill, and who, for a long time, thought of making it his career. As we know, Max Weber was a great scholar but a poor instrumentalist. The only point of comparison among social theorists is Jean-Jacques Rousseau. This introduces another paradox. However, there are surprising similarities in the work of these two men: their care for the elegance of their writing; the variety of their publications; and the mixed reception of their work – Rousseau divided his readers as much as Becker, albeit along different lines.

The oddities accumulate as we examine Becker's career. He does not seem to have any obvious area of specialization, no empirical turf that he owns, no secret theoretical garden that he protects. It would be presumptuous to impose one on him. Nevertheless, his contributions have shaped many fields of study: art, culture, medicine, educational practice, the status and organizations of professions, and the working methods of the human sciences. Touching on everything, he flits from one topic to another, venturing boldly away from the usual routes and rejecting the kind of specialization that is generally the key to lasting professional recognition. He constantly challenges the names and boundaries of specialties. Why has the sociology of education confined itself to the study of schools and other formal sites of learning? Is there not a form of education in learning the skills of social interaction? How do novice criminals learn their trades? Should we not think of learning a new sport as a kind of education? The sociology of the school should open itself to all forms of learning and not just those treated as legitimate by the organization.

How is it possible to present a body of work that is so rich and so varied? What thread can a commentator follow in seeking the key unifying ideas within the diversity of these publications? Is this why so few people have tried to explain Becker's thinking, particularly while he is still alive and productive, and able to contradict or dispute their accounts? Some people do not think that any intelligible synthesis can be produced from Becker's work. They are content simply to read his books, to smile at them and, at best, to cite them without following his example. They cannot imagine taking a lead from him and developing original research modelled on his approach. Its transmission to another generation seems, then, to be impossible.

Becker's concepts have passed into the common sense of the discipline. They form part of a body of research that has still not been fully translated into French, although it is accessible in numerous other languages. His books are studded with observations, enriched by feedback from their readers, just as a musician develops his art in collaboration with his audience. He tests his ideas through direct engagement with his audience. He believes in simple tools, in the interactional foundation of knowledge, and in the durability of solid techniques rather than ethical commitments. This is definitely a strange author who sets out paradoxical ideas – that an excess of methodological sophistication can mean death to rigor! He has declared loudly and clearly that we should no longer use jargon in sociology.

We should write in a more lively fashion. Our model should not be that of a great symphony but of a little sonata, sketching a cartoon or an etching rather than a grand portrait. Ultimately, at the height of his iconoclasm, whether out of false or true modesty, he approaches his own discipline as a social discourse among others, rationalized and with its own specific character (Becker 2007a).

Sociology is a literary form that has its own principles, its own logic, and its own respected conventions. It was invented, he notes, at the same time as photography, in 1838. This is not a mere coincidence for Becker. It is why he puts everything on the same level: novels, geography, mathematics, algebra, journalism, statistics, and cinema. He does not make sociology the queen of the sciences, somewhere above the fray. In a further act of heresy, he opposes the scientism embodied particularly in sociology's elastic approaches to questions of proof. He sets himself against both fetishes and naïve beliefs in demanding equal treatment for all research materials – graphics, photographs, statistical tables, technical vocabularies, field notes or other means of recording data. In so doing, he has changed our traditional topics for inquiry and the way in which we think about arts, science, and humanities.

1

WHY SHOULD WE READ HOWARD BECKER?

When we read original and innovative writers, we open ourselves to the creation of new forms of sociological discourse. This is not a paradox. Such authors invite us to develop our own scholarship as their work takes us beyond our discipline's conventional thinking. The pool of ideas about the social world is inexhaustible. Sociology cannot possibly claim that it has a monopoly: we have always been enriched by our borrowings from geography, history, political economy, arts and letters, and anthropology. Thanks to this openness, we can contrast our characteristic approaches with theirs, assessing the strengths and weaknesses of our own practices and working methods. Such comparisons are a sign of our own health and vigor. Consequently, it seems important to investigate how authors in the social sciences generate new ideas.

What is a new idea in the social sciences? A successful idea seems obvious once someone has formulated and disseminated it. Such novelties are not common in the social sciences. Routine thinking, the intervention of editors, and the inertia of today's aging readership put brakes on change. Paradigm shifts are slowed. These factors all weigh in the direction of conformism and come with a cost: repetitive work, desperate attempts to copy "successful" models, fear of innovation. Through working with Becker, I have come to a better understanding of how deference and docility are embedded within the structures of contemporary sociology. Sociological apprenticeships generally promote this model. The slow pace of professional turnover and renewal locks us into the orthodoxies of the previous century, strangling us with a set of rules that were relevant in a distant past. The burdens of tradition lead sociologists to publish anodyne reports or trivial statements because they are afraid to be adventurous or to take risks. This is why we must read, re-read and study Becker as a case in the terms he himself proposes in his own work: *What is a case?* (Ragin and Becker 1992). What indeed? It is true that everyone can make their own preferred selection from Becker's output. Within this diversity, however, there is an indisputable unity of thought which I shall set out through these pages. Whatever else it may achieve, I hope that this text will serve those with a general interest in sociology by revealing some little-known aspects of the ways in which sociologists create concepts and provide a context for understanding the conditions under which new explanations may appear. It is the lack of such conditions that is causing so many problems at a time when there is an urgent need to join in the analysis of the society that is emerging around us.

Finally, any summary of Becker's work must also take account of some particular characteristics. The author being studied is still very active and internationally recognized. Although these are academic criteria, he is, in many countries, the contemporary sociologist who is most widely published, cited, and translated, on a par with Erving Goffman, while the impact of Robert Merton and Pierre Bourdieu has declined since their deaths, and that of Anthony Giddens since his retirement. Anyone writing about a living author is taking a risk because their body of work has not yet come to an end. Becker's continuing publications confirm this – four books since 2006.[1] The balance sheet is not yet closed. Nevertheless, we can at least introduce and describe his thinking as it is today, throwing light on a diffuse and widely dispersed set of publications.

My interpretation of Becker's thinking is not an authorized or officially sanctioned version. It does not defend a "true" Becker against supposedly false readings. There are as many readings as readers, at least if one applies his own approach, in *Telling about Society* (Becker 2007a), to the reception of a work. None of these readers is wrong. Moreover, like any commentator, I will display my own personal, and independently formed, preferences. This is inevitable. Nevertheless, I have had lengthy discussions with Becker about my own reactions to his work, and the ways in which I have used it.

I will also refer in passing to what Becker has brought to our scholarly generation, and what we have selected from this, made use of, added to, and embedded into our thinking. Every era reads an author through the lenses and questions of its own immediate concerns. We must, then, take account of the need to explain this context to current students, who may not fully understand where Becker has come from, and where he is taking them. They may well ask "Who is this Becker? We often hear him talked about but we do not really study him in our classes, with the possible exception of *Outsiders*" (Becker 2008). Even this book is more cited in student essays than used by active researchers. These are reasonable questions for beginners, who are taught sociology through the accumulation of "epistemologies" or the piling up of themes and schools. In selecting certain aspects of Becker's work, I have tried to focus on useful questions, particularly at a time when we are concerned about the future of the social sciences. Our disciplines are searching for a new direction in the face of public crises – in the recruitment of students and in the confidence of our readers.

If I am not introducing the "authentic" Becker here, this does not really matter. I am describing "our Becker" – a great investigator over sixty years of fieldwork, who has practiced according to his own methods and techniques, with little regard for other people's standards or conventions. It is a position that should engage those younger readers whose competence has yet to be certified. In following Becker, they can avoid over-complicating their investigations, subjecting themselves to the pain, which he rarely takes seriously, of searching for an original topic. His model is one of cultivating a permanent curiosity about everyday life, realized through observation.

Becker's Career

A Series of Simple Precepts

Becker is a pragmatic sociologist with practical goals. A diverse collection of books stands to his account. He has, we might say, led several "careers" – teacher, researcher, investigator, musician, photographer. What does it mean to say that he has "practical and useful goals"? If sociology does nothing to improve your understanding of your own immediate circumstances – to revise your understanding of everyday life and your passage through it – then it has served you poorly.

But Becker gives us other practical advice. For example: "Never commit yourself to a single profession, try several trades at the same time"; "Always write with care, with attention to style"; "Do not exaggerate small differences – do not write a polemic about a minor disagreement just to make a name for yourself". You will encounter these precepts as you work through the following pages – and many other tips, if you read Becker himself. This is not just advice for those who want to get a degree: it is for those who want to practice sociology independently, to make sense of their everyday life, using the discipline as a way to understand the world around them. If you do not want to do that, whether as a student or as a reader, then Becker will be of no use to you.

Is it possible to find any unifying theme in the work of someone who has been an innovator in so many diverse settings? A body of work needs an audience, an organization to promote its diffusion. Innovations need organizations to welcome and disseminate them. Most fail and disappear. For Becker, the business of sociology resembles the music business, with a whole service industry producing manuals, dictionaries, summaries, and media commentaries:

> Well, you have to be innovative in science, too. If I do the same study that you do and get the same result, no one is very interested. Everybody says it's very good to replicate studies, but nobody believes it. Nobody wants to be the one who did the replication. You want them to say: "Müller found" not "Becker found and Müller also found". So it's more a question of what's regarded as innovative. There are people who make changes and everybody says "Oh, you're right", not a problem, and then someone does something else that is a big problem for everybody. It happens in all kinds of communities, especially in the arts. The new book that Rob Faulkner and I just finished is about the jazz repertoire and innovations and what goes into the jazz

repertoire and innovations may be very upsetting to a lot of people.[2] Even though, yes, of course, everybody wants to be individual and unique but not so unique.

(Müller, 2009)

Note that Becker does not attach much weight to the claims made by scientists. They become, instead, the topic of a serious analysis of the diversification and proliferation that is necessary to take the work forward. "Institutions," he has said "are not everything: there are many professors of sociology who do not do sociology and many excellent sociologists who are not employed as professors." His concept of career plays down the element of vocation and insists on the role of chance. As this implies, many career opportunities – some of them possibly "deviant" – offered themselves to him, as to any young person. The first advice that he gives to any beginner is to "stay independent and trust your own abilities. You have a vision, even a small one, of your corner of the world. Your own experience will open doors for you. Make use of it!" Of course there is a price to be paid for taking such liberties with the normal criteria of scholarship. Hard work and application are required to meet Becker's standards and the benefit only becomes apparent after several years of practice.

These are the recommendations of an American scholar, brought up in a university system that was quite open and "democratic" in his youth, working in new fields of social science where entry and promotion had not yet become ossified. They are easier to realize in the United States, which has its own ways of valuing the work of sociologists. The twenty thousand sociologists in the United States are dispersed and independent: they are not regulated and controlled. Today, as we face a decline in funding and recruitment for our discipline, Becker appears as a distinctly contemporary author through his oblique perspective on the times we live in. His conception of our project is sobering. We must read his work as a response to debates about the rights and duties of sociologists in public activism, about the mission of our profession, and about the life of an educator.

Howard Becker's Intellectual Journey

For the purposes of this account, we can divide Becker's life and publications into three main phases:

(1) The years 1950–1970. This is the period of his major empirical works and the various articles collected in *Sociological Work* (Becker 1970). Initially, like other students, the young Becker established his financial independence. From the age of sixteen, he paid for his studies by working as a pianist in bars (seven hours a night, forty-five minutes on, fifteen minutes off). At the same time as he was embarking on the life of a musician, he enrolled in the sociology department of a great university, the University of Chicago, which was then acquiring the reputation that would mark its history as *The Chicago School*. [3]

A precocious talent, Becker defended his PhD thesis at the age of twenty-three, while publishing several articles at the same time. In 1963, he produced his first book, *Outsiders* (Becker 2008), which has been translated into eight languages and become a global point of reference for sociologists. It must be said that he was completely in tune with the culture of that period. He anticipated the universal diffusion of jazz and the spread of counter-cultural movements. He began, like many others, as a researcher without a permanent position, surviving on temporary contracts. Universities had few tenure-track openings at that time and research was a way to keep his career alive while waiting for an opportunity. His postdoctoral employment proved to be a fertile period for research and rich in other experiences, such as editing journals or correcting articles for publication.

(2) The books of the 1980s and 1990s combined his major project on art worlds with several works on the practice of sociology, where he urged colleagues to renounce their pompous academic mannerisms (e.g. *Doing Things Together* [Becker 1986]). This was the most traditional part of his career, as a professor at Northwestern University in Evanston, a suburb of Chicago, where he worked for thirty-four years. He loved teaching. Like his colleagues, he would spend hours in his office at the disposal of his students, talking freely with them, as I observed on many occasions. As for administrative duties in this private university, he only accepted those that he considered to be legitimate: to be reliable in his courses, his examinations and his seminars (but, in a characteristically personal touch, although the courses were delivered, they did not necessarily take place in the advertised locations but in the basement among the maintenance crew!). He broke with the traditional organization of space in classes, where students traditionally face their teacher, symbolically signaling the intellectual hierarchy of the professor speaking from the pulpit or the podium of the lecture theatre. The work that he required from students left space for them to express their independence and avoided signs of authority by grading in broad categories. He resisted evaluations, judgments, and classifications as premature verdicts on young people in the process of learning. Harsh marking for students was inappropriate, particularly given the lack of consensus within sociology about its mission and standards.

(3) Becker's third career is now in progress through his final position at Seattle and his current retirement. It has already yielded several original books, often with collective authorship. He has returned to his preferred style, turning his back on irrelevant "courtesy" references, a heavy load of footnotes (which he has never used) and a self-conscious display of erudition. He has innovated as much as in his youth, revisiting his established themes: the value of sociological studies of everyday life; the engagement with other forms of reporting on the social – by novelists, photographers, journalists, statisticians or artists. In this way, he directly attacks the fundamental problem of the nature of sociology. What kind of a discipline is it? Is it a science? If it is, then what kind of a science? If it is a way of describing society through the multiplication of subtle abstractions, is it any more than a branch of philosophy?

The identification of these three careers is important for French readers because the usual accounts of his work give an impoverished and limited version of Becker's contribution. He has been presented successively as:

a   A sociologist of deviance who anticipated the leisure activities of affluent, urban, middle-class young people, the service industries that have grown up around these, and the alternative ways of life that promised a better future (drugs, music, student cultures). This is the commonest summary of his work in the textbooks.

b   A sociologist of the professions, and of art, whose works treated these sacred and prestigious institutions as if they were mere trades. This body of work takes a more classical form, although it introduces some novel features in its presentation, particularly in the use of photographs or images.

c   Finally, in retirement, Becker is seen as a tester of ideas, a stylistic innovator, a sociologist freed from any institutional role that might oblige him to advise students about how to adapt their practices to the norms and traditions of the university. These late texts can be read as the fruits of years of serenity, written without aggression or the distracting critique of professional rivals. Nevertheless, the velvet language cloaks a steely mind.

Who, then, are we going to meet in the pages that follow? A pragmatic sociologist or a free-ranging scholar? Becker is, above all, a hard worker, focused on his thinking, preserving time for this by keeping his distance from the demands of marketing and self-promotion: "I am never going to be on the radio," he says. "I never go on television. It is a waste of time." His taste for liberty is deep-rooted. Remember that he was financially independent from the age of eighteen as a worker in the night-time economy. These experiences are not affectations but the basis of a great education in the school of life that led to a wide range of investigations and to his understanding of the ephemeral nature of public assessments of success or failure.

I didn't have any trouble in graduate school because, I tell people, I never worried about school, because it was simply a pastime, it was a hobby. The serious business was playing the piano. So I didn't choose sociology, I just kept doing it and then, one day, I had a Ph.D., not trying very hard, not because I am brilliant, but because all my colleagues were worrying and worrying just because they were very serious. If you don't worry it's not that difficult to go through graduate school successfully. And then I realized two things. One is the kind of music business I was in was probably not such a wonderful thing to do forever, because the people I worked for were small time criminals, you know, Mafiosi, and so on, and that probably wasn't good, and the things that would be more successful weren't really so interesting, like writing music for advertising, which I think I could have done very well. So I thought, well, maybe I should try sociology, which I did, and in the same way, you know, you don't choose these things, you do something and that leads to something else...

(Müller, 2009)

Elsewhere, Becker has said:

I became a sociologist by chance, or better by accident...in general, I find it difficult to take on the role of an intellectual, of a great thinker, which people sometimes ascribe to me...music has influenced my sociology. Music helps to give me anthropological distance, the skeptical perspective on the organization and practices of a society that is essential for a sociologist. But I must make an important point. You should not think that I do not take the business of being a sociologist very seriously, even when I am not really being serious about the institutional structures with which this is linked...My work, my research, both are really important to me: but the title and status of a professor and the social roles professors are expected to play...I am not always sure about them! All this, the academic discipline of sociology, the profession of professors, the prestige, the status, doesn't seem at all serious to me. If all of that were to pass away, it would not be the end of the world: if there were no more music in the world, that would be a real tragedy.

But because I wasn't particularly bothered about my hobby – doing sociology – I was able to finish my studies very quickly. So I defended my thesis at the age of 23 years. The serious and conscientious students took very much longer...My thesis was about elementary school teachers. Then I had the problem that no-one would hire me as a university teacher because they thought I was too young. From another point of view, I had become the most credentialed jazz pianist in Chicago. I picked up a job in the year after my thesis, a job with an agency studying delinquency in Chicago. And I persuaded them to let me do this study of marijuana use. However, in the middle of that year, a great storm hit Chicago, a great winter storm, and it brought down an old streetcar on top of a car driven by a university professor, who was very seriously injured. So they suddenly needed a professor. That's how I came to be accepted to teach at the university. That's all there is to it. This story finally made me question the idea of determinism...such a string of coincidences and chances. So I did that research and then I got a postdoctoral fellowship at the University of Illinois. And that's how it all started.

(Bourmeau and Heurtin, 1997)

Although his professional career became linear, Becker's choice of topics and his research interests have been eclectic. This diversity makes discussion difficult: if we isolate one field of study, we end up with a partial understanding of his work; if we try to encompass everything, we can get lost. However, we can draw up this list of the principal themes of his scholarly contribution:

a   Schooling, professional training, and primary or secondary education;
b   Culture – professional practice in art, music, theatre, popular song, and photography;
c   Norms, deviance, social control, transgressions, innovations. This is the aspect of Becker's work that has dominated the reductive approaches and interpretations adopted by many commentators on his biography;
d   The techniques of sociological work, the construction of data and the modes of writing.

We can see the challenges of navigating the ocean of Becker's sociology! He has brought his imagination into play almost everywhere. The principle is simple. In each book, there is one big idea, whose tendrils are traced to their tips. This variety is the result of his refusal to accept the kind of specialization that makes everything routine. The objective of his career has never been to win a following by staying the same forever but to constantly renew himself and to spread the spirit of originality, opening doors through which others might go.

How Did a Chicago Kid Come to Sociology?

If we ask Becker about the origins of his interest in sociology, he gives us a few clues in describing the material and cultural circumstances around his teenage years. In effect, he applies the pragmatic approach to his own life through the construction of these sorts of stories:

> When I was perhaps ten, my boy friends and I would take advantage of the structure of the Chicago elevated train system (the El, everyone called it that) to pay one fare and ride all day long. Our mothers would pack us a sandwich and we would [take off] to the Loop...Once you got on a train, you could find places where the lines crossed – especially in the Loop – and change to another train that went to another part of the city...And do that all day long, covering the entire city, before we went home, tired and happy. What did we see?...As we rode we observed, looking closely at everything that went by our little window on the city, commenting to each other about what we saw, seeing the differences and taking them home with us to think about. By the time I was, say, twelve, I had a good understanding of the physical and social structure of the city, at least from a geographic point of view...My opportunities for observation increased a lot when I was a little older and became a professional musician, which happened before I had ever heard of sociology and well before I entered graduate school in sociology...I was fourteen or fifteen when I began to play with other people in public or semi-public places and get paid for it...Though I still lived with my parents, I was no longer there very much, my time being spent either in school or in the places where I played. All the places I played in were sites of observation, though I didn't

think of them that way, and didn't think that I was doing anything as important or grand as "observing." I was just "living."

(Becker 2009a)

Childhood experiences like these shaped Becker's intellectual openness and curiosity – the observation of a great metropolis, the crowds and trades of its streets, its famous department stores, and its public life, just as much as the private life glimpsed through the windows of the trains on the elevated tracks. The development of this early sense of how to observe an environment may be stimulated or repressed, depending on the way children are brought up in families of different social classes. My generation learned a great deal just wandering around during the school holidays with our little gang of friends. Such a life is hardly imaginable today except for children living in housing projects or so-called "problem areas." The freedom of movement for middle-class children has been greatly restricted. Families have boundaries that have imposed a morality of secrets and shyness. But learning how to visit one's own city as if a stranger or tourist, to watch its inhabitants, to wrap oneself in silence while in the middle of a crowd ("I never listen, I look around," said Diderot at the same age[4]) are the very foundations of social science. In short, to the extent that curiosity is encouraged or constrained by parental or other restrictions, it can feed or starve the sense of inquiry that is the precursor to sociology.

Becker was born in Chicago at the end of the 1920s, a time of great economic crisis. His parents were middle-class employees, living in Austin, a western suburb, inhabited by people like them from Jewish and Irish backgrounds (who all voted Democrat, he said). At high school, he won a scholarship to the university through a very selective, city-wide examination (ten places were supported at the University of Chicago by a Jewish philanthropist). A teacher encouraged him to take the examination, although his father would have liked him to take up a career in the law and not in sociology! Accepted into the university at the age of sixteen, he rapidly progressed to his bachelor's degree in social sciences at the age of eighteen – completing the course requirements in two years rather than three with studies in classical literature, social science, and natural sciences. He took his master's degree at twenty and defended his doctoral thesis at twenty-three. His first article was published at the age of twenty-four in the leading journal, *American Journal of Sociology* and three others appeared in the following year.

When I graduated from this low level of playing (at high school), I found work in bars and taverns and strip clubs. One of my first jobs was at McGovern's Liberty Inn, one of a number of strip clubs in a small stretch of North Clark Street. We sat just behind the small stage the girls danced on and looked beyond them to where the customers sat. I watched night after night as men who had come to Chicago for, perhaps, a business convention bought drinks for the dancers and spent thousands of dollars without even getting any sex for it. We occasionally saw someone well known sitting in the back of the club masturbating while the girls took their clothes off...I played at many bars in many parts of the city. In all of them, I sat on a bandstand with two or three other players that let us look down on the bar and the tables beyond it, and watch people drink, get drunk, dance, and gamble. We watched people flirt with each other, we watched fights between two people turn into major brawls, occasionally involving the club owner and the bartender as well as the customers, we watched the owner of the club bribing policemen...Playing in such places eventually took me to almost every part of the city to spend several hours a night watching local life...Most all of this observation from the bandstand took place before I started graduate school. It wasn't undertaken because I was a sociologist and had a reason to be there observing. I was observing because I was there in pursuit of my musical ambitions.

(Becker 2009a)

The Education of an Investigator

As we have seen, Becker was a precocious scholar who rapidly entered into adult life. To describe this as "embarking on a career in sociology" would be somewhat ironic. This course of events was, he says, the result of a string of good luck: good teachers, committed mentors, and a great university – with libraries that never closed, even at night. There was an atmosphere that valued intellectual work and collaboration. He is quite lyrical about the camaraderie among a generation that produced at least fifty of the finest American sociologists. His chance contact with Everett Hughes, known as "the terror of first-year students" was crucial. Hughes was also a pianist and fascinated by Becker's unusual profile: a student for part of his time, without being a dilettante; passionate about the study of society, but also about music. He chose Becker first to replace him in teaching courses during a period of leave and then as a member of a research team. Becker joined a loose and informal community of graduate students. While he never really cut himself off from his roots in the city, he became part of a group with Eliot Freidson, Joseph Gusfield, Donald Roy, Fred Davis, Erving Goffman, and others whose names are less well known. They developed a shared vision of research that indelibly marked the discipline. It has come to be called the "Second Chicago School," whose members readily acknowledged their mutual influences and intellectual debts. They did not see themselves as an intelligentsia in formation but simply as very lucky young people, especially those who had served in World War II and were granted government scholarships to study at this great university.

Such modesty is unfamiliar to us in a world of rugged individualists. However, this quality is evident among these young, post-war, American sociologists, who benefited from an exceptional apprenticeship. In contrast to most European sociologists, their studies were not dominated by classical philosophy.[5] This partly explains some of the differences in approach between the two sides of the Atlantic. Becker's generation of graduate students were not impregnated with either Anglo-Saxon positivism or European rationalism. Certainly, Becker has his own precursors: Robert Park, George Herbert Mead, John Dewey, some of whom had studied philosophy under the banner of Georg Simmel or the pragmatists Charles Sanders Peirce and William James. Is this the core of the distinction between, on the one hand, the philosophically oriented sociology of France or Germany and the pragmatically oriented sociology of the Anglo-Saxon world? Perhaps – in any case these differences can be analyzed historically. They illuminate the reasons for the delayed appreciation of Becker's work in France, and the continuing resistance of the German-speaking world, which has been more favorable to structural approaches.

Becker's recognition in France also coincides with the end of the 1980s which saw the implosion of many of the sects within French sociology and the end of the struggles between their leaders. In the context of this turbulence, it was possible, after 1985, to get a better hearing for Becker's work. Fifteen or so books, of which half have been translated into French, and more than one hundred published papers and notes bear witness to the extent to which he has now conquered a public. Becker is not a vagabond professor, holding multiple positions, although he has moved between Chicago, Seattle, and San Francisco.[6] He does not hesitate to acknowledge that he has been lucky – missing war service because he was too young, for example. "Becoming a seriously grown-up person is a complicated business," he says. Becoming a consummate professional is just the same kind of adventure. Apprentices have to discover the solutions that their seniors hide more or less carefully from them. In order to ease this passage, he himself has tried to provide more explicit guidance to his own successors. Giving beginners a guide to the "tricks of the trade," the recipes, the workings of the kitchen, all of this is intended to convince them that there are no revolutionaries or geniuses – in sociology or anywhere else. You can learn the trade of a researcher, but first you need to understand how it really works and what the constraints are.

We began this chapter by asking why we should read Howard Becker. We now have the beginnings of an answer. Considering the scale of his work, the variety of his contributions, the flexibility of his thought, the twists and turns of a researcher's career, we can sense that he is not given to being a grand-master of scholarship, that he refuses to be straitjacketed as the leader of a methodological school. In the course of his work, he has never burdened himself with rigid rules or tried to present a pale imitation of scientific methods. We are misled if we think it is necessary that serious and scholarly work follows the models of social philosophy or, at the other extreme, adopts the systems and lexicons of mathematical physics.

Now, if someone asks us, whether from genuine or false curiosity, "Why should we read Becker?", we can reply without hesitation: "To liberate us!"

All of this has been well put by Alain Pessin (2017), who found exactly the right title for his book – *A Sociologist on the Loose*, especially in his chapter six, "A Researcher Set Free," which underlines Becker's sense of humor, a commodity in short supply within our profession.[7]

Notes

1 A further book, *Evidence*, was published in 2017 (Becker 2017). This is discussed in the Editor's Introduction.
2 The reference is to Faulkner and Becker (2009).
3 Peneff is referring to what is more generally known as the Second Chicago School that emerged after World War II. Although there is a clear legacy from the First Chicago School of Park, Burgess, Thomas, and others, the focus is on a different generation of scholars (Fine 1995).
4 The reference is to the French philosopher, Denis Diderot (1713–1784). The quotation ("je n'écoute jamais, je regarde") comes from line 62 of an unfinished dramatic work of 1768, *Mystification ou histoire des portraits*. See Diderot (1964).
5 See the discussion in the Editor's Introduction about the links between sociology and philosophy in French universities after World War II.
6 This refers to the propensity of French professors to hold multiple appointments (see note 6 in Introduction), which is attributable to the degree of institutional separation between teaching and research in French higher education. It also reflects relatively liberal approaches to releasing senior faculty from their duties in France to allow them to work regularly in other countries, without requiring them to resign their French positions.
7 This is my translation of the French title of Pessin's book, published in 2004. The US translation has a quite different title (Pessin 2017).

2

THE SOCIOLOGIST OF WORK

The Division of Labor, Occupations and Institutions

It is not easy to describe such a diverse body of writing as that produced by Howard Becker, even if it is so clearly expressed. Each page makes sense the first time you read it. There is no hermetic obscurity. His studies of work may, though, be a good place to start.

Whether through the economic forces of wages or salaries, or through the impact of organizations, the world of work is the most important influence that shapes our futures, classifies us, and inspires our actions. Becker became interested in the study of work because he likes to see people in action, the variety of their contributions, and the ingenuity they bring to their labors.

Work is at the center of life in all societies. It lies at the heart of every activity. It is the great organizing principle of social existence. Without work, there would be no society – and, of course, no sociology (Hughes 1971: 338–347; see also pp. 298–303). We frequently forget this when we are teaching undergraduates. If there is a course in the sociology of work, it often ends up being sub-contracted rather than taught by core faculty. But work is always a collective enterprise. The strength of individualist thinking in our society leads us to underestimate the organizational aspects of human labor. We can only challenge this preconception by seeking out the times and places where it is possible to penetrate the boundaries around the supposedly most personalized occupations: education, medicine and art. These are the locations where the work of a team as a community of equals is devalued in favor of a hierarchy of merit or an individualization of capacities. All these sites have been explored by Becker since the early days of his career. His utilitarian vision of society has led him to use the same language to talk about jazz, marijuana, photography, and theatre as to discuss education, medicine, or the training of sociologists. Before we look at this contribution in detail, however, we must return briefly to Becker's place within sociology's short history. Many commentators have wanted to classify him as a qualitative sociologist, as an interactionist, or as a member of the Chicago School. All these labels are wrong.

Becker as a Victim of "Labeling"

Sociologists tend to learn a way of categorizing their work as they are socialized into their own professional community and learn its codes of practice, whether through a formal curriculum or their career experience. This may help students to master the subject more quickly but it comes at a cost. The delayed translation of *Outsiders* (Becker 2008) into French, for example, has shaped Becker's image, and subsequent choices about other work to translate.[1] His major investigations of education and medicine have been neglected. Although *Outsiders* is an important book, French sociologists have been diverted away from Becker's treatment of fundamental institutional questions. It almost reverses his own career, where, at the age of 30, he wrote several key methodological statements opposing the functionalism that dominated US sociology until the 1970s. Our disciplinary history in France is different: which is why he has been translated as an after-thought. While his membership of the Chicago School is presented as self-evident – which is disputable – our traditions of compartmentalization have labelled him as a specialist in deviance or sub-cultures, or even as a champion of interactionism, although his own work defies such classifications. We have assimilated him as a practitioner of qualitative research (which is true), although this is countered by his concern, in *Tricks of the Trade* (Becker 1998), for questions of sampling, of case studies and of comparative analysis. His working methods have never become settled and stable. They are fluid and evolve to match their subjects. He has never allowed himself to be influenced by prior definitions of what constitutes a "field." Nor has he been concerned to define and justify observational data. His first contribution, "labeling theory," was a study of moral entrepreneurs, and other people who claimed moral authority. How did they bring facts together and assemble them into patterns of conduct to be judged by specialists in moralizing – police officers, legislators, journalists, and crusaders? How did these people jointly decide whether or not some activity should be classified as deviant? All this went on under the influence of sociologists, and other professionals, whose role was to describe society in terms of "social facts" that were supposedly objective but were morally loaded. It may seem obvious today that statistics are socially constructed and that there is an implicit process of labeling in the actions of artists, doctors, educators and others: in 1950, it was barely the germ of an idea. Nevertheless it was a new idea that inspired the researchers of his generation.

For Becker, talking about potheads and druggies is already deviant. In medicine, the "bad patient," who has caused their own illness and behaved like a pain in the ass – a "crock" in medical slang – reframes in local terms the way in which society makes moral judgments about health. For the police and the criminal justice system, "deviant" is almost directly equivalent to delinquent. We sociologists, however, must justify the language that we use to describe the people we study. The chosen term is never innocent. *Outsiders* was intended to identify those who are, ultimately, adopting other, competing, ways of life: in the margins, on the sidelines but not necessarily devalued, excluded or criminalized.

Fields and Experiences

From its earliest days, sociology established itself mainly, although not exclusively, through observational research. Every movement in the history of the social sciences has developed its own frameworks for making judgments and recommendations (Chapoulie 2001; Masson 2008). Each field of study develops its own techniques. It would be wrong to constrain or limit these. Nevertheless, we can note the lack of concrete empirical investigations relative to the proliferation of theories. What makes a research site useful is the initial knowledge that one brings to it. Without previous experience, any site is a desert. We must either possess or acquire some experience before beginning fieldwork. Not everyone can do this. But the problem is not insurmountable: we can learn how to observe and begin at any age. "The field" is not predetermined. The skill of learning about it through absorption resembles that of historians working with archives, although they are more distant from their sources and the questions of "objectification" do not arise to the same degree. They do, however, share our concerns with bias and with the naiveté of the researcher.

What does it mean to talk about "making experiences into sociology"? There is a straightforward answer. An inquiring life involves grasping opportunities to learn, testing them out, and being curious, from adolescence right into old age. The essential thing is the number of cases you can collect and the cumulative reasoning you can bring to them. There are many ways of enlarging the pool of experiences if we do not restrict ourselves to being just one kind of observer or one kind of participant. Like Becker, we must be inventive, adaptive, and take risks, stepping out of our social class or career trajectory – studying new things at any age, becoming in our fifties an apprentice in photography or theatre arts, or taking a course in Boolean algebra. These are the sorts of actions that Becker values! This implies that our career strategies should not be too rigid or codified. Chance must also have its place. We must not put participant observation into a straitjacket by predefining the places to go and the time to be spent there. Where, in reality, is "the field"? It is everywhere and nowhere.

This is why Becker, a tireless researcher, has distanced himself from conventional treatments of his chosen topics: jazz, marijuana, photography – each in its time a novel subject for sociology. We must be attentive to changes in the currents of society. Becker would not take on a research topic unless he felt a real desire to investigate and write about it. He does not claim any particular specialization or consistent theme. It would have been a bold call to suppose that the approach to problems that he developed in the 1960s would survive for such a long time, but his research has not aged. Immersing oneself in the flow of everyday life, not standing on the sidelines, imagining a sociology that is practical, reflexive and concerned about contemporary realities – that is what our profession is all about. His concern for what comes next follows from this stance: how can we publish and share our work with the widest audience? Becker's durability as a researcher owes much to the autonomy of our discipline in the United States. This is less politically engaged because the title "professor of sociology" is less respected by journalists and other commentators. US sociologists are also more vulnerable to the risks of insecure positions, especially during the early part of a university career.

Although Becker is a sociologist of work, he does not, then, think that it is essential for sociology to form part of public agencies or to be placed at the service of state institutions. Some members of our profession must always be free to investigate new ideas about society and culture, and the ways in which these are expressed. People have to be able to improvise responses to a world that is restless and volatile. We should not try to make research formulaic and bureaucratic. The process of creation must remain open and embrace unconventional, and even profane, ideas. Sociology is not a science in the hypothetico-deductive sense: it advances in jumps... or by going crabwise. Its experiences cannot be replicated. Becker thinks, then, that traditional methods courses are mistaken. We should simply produce our analyses through the comparison of cases collected from free-ranging observations. The first principles of pragmatism are learning through experience, tested against reality. Just having social experiences, and understanding their material foundations, is not, though, sufficient in itself: the author and the researcher must also go on to communicate them in writing, exchanging ideas with neighboring disciplines.

Sociology textbooks tend to slice up Becker's work because they have difficulty classifying it under a single label. It does not fit into classic, and well-fought over, territories. Becker has only ventured into fields that he knows at first hand, and has studied at length. He is an unusual academic who holds his research apart from the institutionalized university. The boundaries established by such organizations limit the opportunities for exploring the margins of society. Amateurs may know these spaces better and, for this reason, be able to contribute to sociological reflections on their significance.[2] All fieldwork necessarily involves taking risks, whether personal, professional or intellectual. It also requires a certain indifference to whatever a country thinks are the founding texts for its national approach to sociology. The founding texts are only useful to the extent that they help to understand the experience of the field.

Becker emphasizes the contingent nature of careers and knowledge in a discipline like ours. We can illustrate this contingency with the testimony of someone who happened to experience both sides of these educational barriers. Paule Verdet, who graduated from the École Normale Supérieure in 1950, escaped "Parisian Excellence" and went to Chicago to study with Everett Hughes, who was also Becker's dissertation adviser.[3] From a welder in a factory to a professor of sociology in Boston, her career represents the integration of these two modes of knowledge. Without ever making an explicit programmatic statement, Becker puts forward a view of sociology and its practices that contrasts sharply with current fashions. As the new century begins, we should listen to his call to abandon these stale approaches. His later works, which have finally reached us in France, invite us to breathe fresher air.

The Big Projects

Becker's major publications on education, doctors and artists challenge narrow views of science as a universal way of explaining human social organization. For him, the problems that methodologists agonize over are irrelevant because they are insoluble. The idea of "proof" derived from the hard sciences is not applicable. Attempts to import this standard misunderstand scientific practice, where proof is always provisional and findings subject to revision by scientists themselves. The work that we call "sociology," whether or not this is conducted within a university, is justified only by the degree to which it enriches collective reflection or fosters debate on a topic of public interest. The contexts in which we communicate our results are never standardized and uniform. Artificial categories do not capture applications of our work that arise and exist only in the moment.

> That may seem unfortunate, but it is exactly the provisional character of sociological knowledge which identifies it as a true science. Because all scientific knowledge is provisional. Our discoveries and laws all depend on conditions which may seem to us universal, but which further research will inevitably show to be true in the places we know about but not in some other places we have yet to discover. Taking these further possibilities into account as they arise is what keeps sociological science moving, learning from our mistakes, adding more and more to what we know even as we learn, more and more, how little we know.
>
> *(Becker 2007a)*

The Techniques of Work

The diversity of meanings given by societies to the concept of work is not a source of trouble. We should not let ourselves be diverted by *a priori* classifications – this is work, this is a hobby, this is volunteering, this is domestic. Nor should we make assumptions about whether work is humble or prestigious. What is the relationship between playing in a concert, cleaning the hall and selling the tickets? It is obvious: from a societal point of view, art is nothing if the concert or exhibition cannot take place because the hall has not been maintained or the tickets have not been sold.

Practice

Clearly, Becker's practice rests on a foundation: an inductive methodology that starts from facts established by experience. The world of work is the one that he knows best. He takes the view of an employee – whether a musician or a researcher. What can one do as a sociologist who depends upon odd jobs, part-time work or employment on fixed-term contracts? We can turn this handicap to our advantage: sociology is the only social science in this situation. Being employed from the age of sixteen is not a redundant part of our education. On the contrary, it is a fast track to understanding the discipline. Prior experience of the world, whether as an employee or as a migrant adapting to a new culture, is an opportunity to challenge the "scholar-centrism" of most academics, and the barriers between higher education and the world of work, whether in business or elsewhere. We can profit by being teachers who leave our doors open and encourage people to walk through them. Our graduates and their dissertations bear witness to the way in which students can use their experiences to produce quality research. But this does involve a double shift: researcher by day and worker by night (Chapoulie and Tripier 1998; Chapoulie and Briand, 2000).

Rather than being their immediate route into a job, the dissertations written by our students, at all levels, are a real opportunity for these novices to develop their independence. They can build confidence in their grasp of a subject so that, as Becker puts it, the apprentice comes to know it better than their supervisor. More abstract kinds of explanation will follow quite naturally as they make use of concepts: the content of tasks, competition, imitation, negotiation, collaboration, interaction, hierarchy, and labelling. These take the place of the vague notions that authors who lack such concrete data apply unthinkingly: variables, forces, mechanisms, logics, constructions or systems. When someone has experienced this kind of education, they do not expect ready-made explanations. They are committed to the integration of theory and method through techniques such as close observation, the examination of internal documents, and the recording of conversations. Theory and method are the two constituents of the reality of research. Theorists and researchers collaborate and exchange more than they admit to or leave traces of in archives or reports. Co-workers meet and talk to each other. If they do not actually meet, they interact at a distance, imagining each other's reactions and taking account of their anticipated opinions, reactions or strategies. This is the basis of collective action. Becker sets out this approach in quite specific ways in *Doing Things Together* (1986) and in *Sociological Work* (1970). He has applied it widely in studies of elementary schooling, of medicine, and of cultural production, as well as to science and other areas of everyday life.

Comparing the Worlds of Work

Over the last hundred years, the division of labor has exploded. Activities have multiplied, seemingly without end, and there seem to be no limits to the segmentation of work. This is why it is important to add new case studies to those which are already established. We must not be the kind of sociologist whose capacity to do this is paralyzed by the assumption that they are a specialist who has mastered a particular institution or theoretical approach. When we are asked the, implicit or insidious, question, "What is Becker's specialism?", the reply is that he is a specialist in change, in interactions, in variations. Everything is mingled: the tasks that are to be done, their physical or mental requirements, the layout of the workshop or office, the hierarchical distribution of power, and the nature of the organization and its internal controls. Some elements are more important in one site but not in another. Our first task is to understand how these elements are combined in the acts of organizing, planning, and producing whatever output is required. Donald Roy (2006) has made similar points in *Un sociologue à l'usine.* [4]

"Work" is an ill-defined concept in sociology but is usually found as a noun associated with the study of organizations that create employment, jobs and functions. From the beginning, Becker has distanced himself from the definitions adopted for official statistics, administrative structures or organizational charts. He contrasted his approach with that of positivist statisticians who rely on formal classifications and job titles to define the categories recognized by the official division of labor. Work, for Becker, is not the essence of employment. Where, he asks, does work begin and end? When someone walks into or out of the workplace – the office, the factory, the hospital? No. Becker has developed a sociology of activities and occupations based on matrices of actions that are more or less alike. Work is not a generic concept but a relationship that is ambiguous and complex. It is a way of constructing a community through interaction with others. If one is working, this is in a relationship with someone else, and probably also for someone else or against some other person. The fruits of our labor must find a buyer – a user, a consumer or a client. Without a buyer, there can be no social activity, no trade, no organization of work. Society is a chain of workers. The consequence of this approach is to see the series of actions involved in a prehistoric mammoth hunt as potentially comparable to the manufacture of a satellite. Whatever the specific subject that we choose, the linking theme is the way in which an organization's work assembles a collection of actors.

This is not simply a matter of one or two phases. On the contrary, it runs through all the actions of a team of professionals or workers. Becker does not claim to be a complete expert when he adopts the viewpoint of a network of producers, but, drawing also on the experience of his fellow students in Chicago, who drove taxis, worked on assembly lines or in a variety of service jobs, he brought together thirty years of reflections on the range of activities that constituted work. We might bear in mind that, in the 1940s, the University of Chicago had set aside its traditional elitism for a time and, reversing its usual policies, had admitted to its sociology department young people – former soldiers and war workers – with few qualifications but evidence of strong motivation.[5] In order to support studies of industrial work, the university had sought out students with strong personalities and diverse experiences. This exceptional recruitment followed in the footsteps of the former professor, Robert Park, who was appointed at the age of forty-nine, a fine example of someone who came late to sociology and brought a particular imagination to the discipline.[6]

Who Does What, Where and How?

Our society has an ever-present tendency to value individuals at the expense of the collective. Whether in sport, art, politics or journalism, we talk about people as isolated agents. Contemporary culture treats the individual as essential and forgets what is more important: the institutions within which individuals form groups. The resulting discourses, or descriptions of work, confuse both the occasional dabbler and the specialist, those who are focused on the topic and those who are skimming through it: the difference is exactly that of "organization." However informal a group may be, it rests on a basis of statutes, legal rights, contracts and recruitment to assemble a relatively stable set of roles. The comparisons with musical careers are crucial for Becker. The young musician is a worker passing through a succession of roles from apprentice, to mastery of the craft, to experimenter and innovator, and finally to retirement. Whether it is football or music, the same processes are at work. It is enough to elicit the commitment of two million young footballers or boxers to their craft.

When we have defined an area of work to study, the next question becomes "How is it divided up?" We can map the groups that come together or are separated into teams – that sometimes compete with each other, and sometimes form alliances. The study of co-operation and the building of coalitions is a huge, but neglected, field for exploration. This is attributable to our errors in applying abstract theoretical models of hierarchy and domination that characterize individuals as fragmented beings submitting to the alienation of their labor. Career ladders, organization charts, classifications are misleading aggregations. It is co-operation that creates the context for competition and rivalry. Co-operation comes before conflict: unity precedes war. In the course of production, co-operation is the basic driving force for productivity (Becker and Pessin 2017).

Finally, Becker's advice implies that we should never isolate an act, a gesture, or a product but always examine their place within a chain of interactions. Let us take, he says, a stable group of workers who form regular connections. This might be a school class, a scientific laboratory, an orchestra, a law court, a sports team – it does not really matter. When we study such a group, we can see them as a set of connected actions and ask a series of questions: under what authority is someone acting, who are they working alongside (which raises further questions about the social life of the workplace), according to what kind of rules – fixed or flexible? No position in an organization can be described independently of the other positions that it is seen to be engaged with, by the organization's members themselves in their everyday interactions. This, though, rarely happens in our research. Becker asks us to abandon a "god's-eye" point of view. The sociologist should take a place within an organization and describe it from the perspective of the actors in that place – possibly after interviewing them. But the informants are not likely to express spontaneously the idea of the primacy of co-operation, association and alliances, even if competition and rivalry are evident. They will not think that it is an important thing to tell the interviewer. However, for clans or cliques to struggle against each other, they must first create associations, organized centers or gangs. A sociologist who is not familiar with the details of their research site is likely to be misled by its discourse. The necessity of joining forces and assembling coalitions (both Marx and Durkheim insist on the pre-existence of associations or "organic solidarity") is lost to view if an ethnographer does not know the circumstances and conditions of the work she or he is studying. Moreover, if one relies only on interviews or conversations, the weight of the invisible, and perhaps informal, actions of the hierarchy may not be evident. While we sometimes forget the institutional framework for co-ordination, Becker's approach to sociology always looks for the divisions in an organization, the specialization of tasks, and the planning that synchronizes actions. How does he advise us to study co-operation?

After assessing what is practicable, Becker says, choose actors who have a good view of the internal life of the organization, such as a pivotal group of people, workers on the front line or in a strategic position (supervisors, accountants, counter staff, recruiters). Trace their principal relationships with the other groups and categories involved in the provision of the service – producers, purchasers, clients, suppliers and competitors. Select one of these relationships to explore the interactions that give rise to it and to assemble the maximum number of perspectives on the scene. Examine an established relationship by describing a series of repeated events or interactions. Write up your impressions and re-read, and reflect upon, them frequently. This is the first step. But it could be pursued to infinity: expanding, or deepening, by investigating increasingly remote situations in order to better contrast them with those that are at hand. This may seem strange advice but do not be too limited by your chosen case study. You will find surprising results, always suggesting new ideas and perspectives.

Outside the world of work, co-operation still has a recognized place. Families, households, neighborhoods, participants in community or leisure activities, all organize life by means of groups, clusters or teams as a basis for their association. The creation of harmony among these individuals (who have different customs, prejudices and assumptions, as well as varying capacities and eccentricities) is achieved by means of conventions, implicit rules that permit momentary agreements. These conventions, of which we may not be consciously aware, favor, if not exactly harmony, then silent understandings, a kind of unspoken language (like gestures, habits or uniforms). Knowledge is tacitly shared in order to generate joint action. We can see this in Becker's late work on the implicit communication among jazz players (Faulkner and Becker 2009).

The Foundations of the Big Projects

Becker's approach began with a study of elementary school teachers (for his doctoral dissertation) and then a project on medical students, his first point of comparison. During three years in the University of Kansas medical school in Kansas City as a "student-observer," and another three years studying undergraduates in humanities and social science on the university's main campus at Lawrence, Becker worked as part of a team that brought together several generations of professors and graduate students. By comparing elementary school teaching with that in humanities or medicine, he brought out their common elements. The result was the classic monograph, *Boys in White* (Becker et al. 1961), whose influence has continued unabated for more than fifty years since its first publication, reaching eleven editions by 2008. The book had four co-authors: two established professors, Everett Hughes and Anselm Strauss, and two postdocs, Howard Becker and Blanche Geer. This was one of the first fieldwork studies in higher education. For a number of reasons, this book has not been translated into French. Some potential readers would be scandalized by an account of medicine that finds it to be a rather ordinary kind of job with the usual conflicts and mutual incomprehension between teachers and students.[7]

Ethnographic research is threatening when it brings the most prestigious of professional trainings down to the level of commonplace education. This pioneering study describes the unexpected responses of the novices to the authoritarian behavior of their teachers. The students developed an autonomous and defensive culture of their own. Such an opposition is unavoidable, but it comes with a crucial cost. "What do they want us to learn?" ask the students. The problem, reply the researchers, is that their teachers do not know, and do not agree among themselves. Medical knowledge is intrinsically provisional and always changing as a result of scientific discoveries. The medical faculty do not know how to teach something that is so fluid and difficult to structure, in establishing links between symptoms, tentative diagnoses and therapies. They do not teach the process of investigation through interactions with patients so the medical students improvise their own, individual or shared, solutions. One of these spontaneous "student cultures" deals with the uncertainty by reconstructing medical knowledge, as something that can be regurgitated into simple, but effective, exam answers. Of course, this book displeased many physicians, who still ask today: "How can we integrate young people into our profession through an educational program that is indisputably rational?" Everett Hughes already had some anticipation of the influence of medical professors from his previous research on nursing and the impact of medical power on that occupation.[8]

In the spirit of Becker's own work, one could say that the worlds of medicine came before the worlds of art: similar projects on the complex interactions and boundaries between systems and the ways in which these led to failures and redundancies. Becker, who still remembers this part of his career very clearly, pulled out of his observations two classic books and about ten outstanding articles on the nature of educational institutions. All this between the ages of twenty-four and twenty-nine years (Becker 1970).

Another of Becker's important contributions was his approach to the enigma at the heart of the sociology of work. Everyone has their place in the immense division of labor, of which educational institutions form one part. Many analysts have struggled with this mystery: it is a miracle that millions of individuals find a position, a job or an occupation in the enormous range of activities that happen in a given territory, contributing in their small way to an outcome that will broadly satisfy all those who contribute to it – which is not to say that they may not also wish for change or development. How is it that everyone can adapt to their place in formulating their goals and their dreams, adjusting their preferences or dislikes, their strengths and their weaknesses, their desires and their disgusts, their skills and their natural endowments?

Becker attacks this problem with two kinds of data, comparing elementary schools where the challenge is to control working-class children, who may often be disruptive in class, with schools where the challenge is to control middle-class parents, who may be interfering and arrogant. Depending upon the neighborhood where a teacher is working, and the status of the school – private or public, these challenges do not usually need to be managed at the same time because of the social selection of the pupils. Take one action or aspect of the teacher's work, he suggests, and push your thinking to its logical conclusion by means of one simple question: who does this worker depend upon and who is the client or audience for their work? The elementary school teacher sometimes works at her relations with the school principal and sometimes, according to her position, with the parents. At the same time, she also has to improvise teaching methods that are suitable for children from poor families who do not value schooling. In the same way, physicians are supposed to treat all sick people equally, whether they present conditions that interest the practitioner or they are hypochondriacs or malingerers. The criteria that the physicians use to make these distinctions vary according to their role: general practitioners who experience the demands of their clients at the point of entry to the system do not make the same kinds of judgment as the research specialists who are committed to the goal of scientific progress, or the clinicians working in private hospitals, who are entrepreneurs seeking immediate profits. Although the jobs have the same title, the categorizations of sick people, and the implications for the tasks associated with them, are not the same.

Another research project, published under the title *Making the Grade* (Becker et al. 1968) (referring to the professorial activity of marking assessments and awarding degrees) has been through five reprints and become another standard text. Becker has continued to explore its themes in revising the preface, particularly in the most recent (1995) edition. He has maintained his interest for more than fifty years because of his discovery of two professions (teachers and doctors) whose expert status rests, to some extent, on the political impact of their rights and duties. Teaching the young or learning how to care for the sick are activities that show how the concept of "work" is not limited to tasks that have been planned or assigned. The content of professional work must constantly be reinterpreted because the conditions under which it is performed are so variable. The "clients" also have their own ideas. Becker learned an early lesson from inverting conventional assumptions about the technical or moral framing of professional work. Sociologists must free themselves from such taboos and develop their own categorizations of work. Even if the work is sometimes illegal, this does not matter because it can still reveal the nature of "professional" concerns. A thief follows his trade, whether seriously as a true "professional" or as an amateur, in managing its risks. Every trade – even that of thievery – has its own internal hierarchy, its own ways of classifying actions (Sutherland 1937). Work may be legitimate or illegitimate, prestigious or humble but the same sociological concepts and analyses can be applied.

> Most people think that burglary is something that demands great courage. In actual fact, the thief really does not want to prove his bravery: the display of virility does not interest him. What he wants above all is a quiet working day…burglars want to be sure that they are not going to encounter anyone. They want…to know in advance who will buy their goods and at what price; to enter the house, recognize what is worth the trouble of carrying off and leave the house; to put the merchandise somewhere safe and to sell it on; finally to return home with the profits of the day. As I was saying, all this demands common sense to carry out all these activities. It is an example of the complexity of work that makes observation necessary; we cannot be satisfied with a few fragments of information on the topic
>
> *(Interview with Becker in Briand and Peretz 1996, p. 66).*

He takes this analogy further.

> One can say the same things about a professional criminal, like a burglar. If we understand in detail the real nature of his activities, we cannot think of him as we often do – marked by the traits of a deviant, someone, for example, who is psychologically disturbed. This kind of crime is a very complex activity, which demands careful preparation and relations with a complicated social network: "colleagues", informers, fences and dealers, often even police officers. It is difficult to imagine that someone who was mentally disordered could really carry out all these negotiations and plans. You need to be calm, with all your wits about you, in order to be able to carry out this profession, as with any other…I think that we spend too much time researching the exceptional cases, even though these have played an interesting part in the development of sociological thought…the study of everyday categories is of fundamental importance. Take a category like that of "delinquent"; it is absolutely commonplace in some sectors of society, or, better, the individuals whose behavior could lead them to enter into this category are widespread…people are constantly breaking many laws, such as those related to driving cars, for example.
>
> *(Interview with Becker in Briand and Peretz 1996, pp. 66–67)*

Becker claims that he came to understand sociology thanks to his parallel career as a musician. Why does he emphasize this second trade, not as a hobby, not as a leisure activity but as another real job? His prime reason is probably his desire as a sociologist not to be cut off from the activities, the economic realities and the everyday conditions of ordinary workers. His second trade is a permanent site for fieldwork, and for the testing of his hypotheses.

The Music Business

What has jazz done for Howard Becker? This music in all its shapes and forms, its lexicon and its semantics, pervades his work. His metaphors, his images, his examples, draw constantly on this point of reference. He describes an analytic reflection as a "Coda" (Becker 1998, p. 215); he often cites ethnomusicology, on which he is an expert; he proposes to "fix our ears" and urges us to re-read our work out loud in order to detect the false notes. In *Writing for Social Scientists* (Becker 2007b), he denounces stylistic faults, vague terminology, excessive use of passive forms, and inappropriate abstraction – all through musical allusions (see especially Chapter 4 which is full of examples).

Many intellectuals took up a passion for jazz as an introduction to modernity after World War II. Our culture has since been invaded by music. In a number of his writings, Max Weber (1958) compared the written music of the West with the oral music of popular traditions as components of a universe of sound. Jazz has inspired many historians and sociologists. From his encounters, Eric Hobsbawm (1998) created a "sociology of jazz," and included his critical writing on concerts in a book called *Uncommon People: Resistance, Rebellion and Jazz*.

As well as a source for inspiring research and pedagogy, Becker uses music as one of his "tricks of the trade" for introducing logic, justificatory reasoning and the concept of a repertoire into the world of sociology. A group of sociologists – a microsociety in effect – resembles a jazz band, whose members come together, challenge each other, collaborate and compete in a flexible organization, whose work includes an element of improvisation. In our lives, we are players: we are presented with what is permitted, an authorized degree of improvisation. The tempo of our lives, their register, their style, are fixed in advance but not completely. Jazz is often said to be half written and half oral: it is not that everything is allowed, but that what is allowed offers sufficient space to be creative. The encounter between sociology and jazz in France was a matter of chance. However, it has established itself to the point of creating local traditions (in Toulouse, for example, sociologists like Marie Buscatto, Marc Perrenoud and Marc Suteau inherited jazz, played with it and sang with it).

Like musicians, sociologists study melody, its construction, and its engagement with the tastes and preferences of its audience. They reach an agreement with their peers about the choice of register, the selection of tonality, and the overall plan of the piece, as well as its style and the order of speakers or players. The moments for solos and choruses emerge much as a band reacts to a musician. For Becker, participation in music is a symbol of life in society: each of us plays their part in a score that weaves individual contribution into a general fabric.

This is more than a metaphor: it is almost a theory, an organizing schema, a method of analysis, which Becker has taken to the greatest height. He has repeated this on many occasions – but we have not paid enough attention. Nevertheless, he has continued because it was so obvious to him. This is why Becker the musician is so important for understanding Becker the sociologist. He has introduced jazz to the perspective of the sociology of work (Becker 2008, pp. 101–119). While it is essential to understand how a group of professionals deals with their work situation, sociology has more to say than this. When someone plays the piano in the evening, they have to satisfy the requirements of multiple audiences: the peers who make up the band; the event's promoter; the management of the venue; the suppliers of the scores; the vendors and tuners of the instruments; the sound technicians, without even considering the administrators of the intellectual property rights or the unions that provide the membership card that licenses the performer. When we talk of an artist, we must see behind them tens of dependents, collaborators and decision-makers. The assessments of these third parties are critical. The weight of their judgment is built on the credibility of the sanctions available to them, or the gratifications and rewards that flow from the users of the service. The quality of the service is judged in the light of the perceptions and feelings of the public: this is even more the case when the assessment of the performance is almost simultaneous and tied to the moment, as with sport, art and personal services.

We can see similar issues in thinking about artists who must work to become recognized. They may spend more time on "communication," or self-promotion, than in their studio, where, sheltered from critical views, they can create artworks. Where does the labor of the artist begin and end? It is difficult to say because there are so many grey areas that are hidden from our sight. Among physicians, the process of recognition is subtle. Novices must abandon their initial ideals of providing "care for all" and adopt a mixture of cynicism and practical realism (one cannot cure everyone – far from it – but the pretense must be maintained). They learn the role of a good student, and then that of a dutiful intern.

Becoming a seasoned professional signifies the application both of norms that are unknown to the public and the unmistakable signs of competence. How can a doctor preserve their own autonomy of practice? How can a professional conscience be protected while closing one's eyes to the diagnostic errors or failures of an incompetent colleague – or of one's own? The appropriate response is not a public accusation. Such restraint is endorsed by most colleagues, in the interests of maintaining public respect for the profession, and protecting oneself against reciprocal allegations of failure or fraud. When you are doing the job, you have to learn all the things that medical school did not teach you. This, in fact, is almost everything. The school only teaches the bare minimum of abstract knowledge, conferring a professional title and the outward signs of expertise. These are the basis of the self-assurance to reply to complaints from the users of your services. Graduation in itself generates the credibility that is the foundation of a physician's legitimacy in dealing with sick people and their families.

This way of looking at the process of education is taken over from the world of entertainment. How does learning go on between peers? How do we evaluate the norms that are laid down by one's professors or the music professionals who hire us? How should we react to the tastes of the listeners or examiners? Every novice has to deal with these questions. How does one enter or leave a "business," that amalgam of publics, sponsors, critics, recruiters, directors or deans of faculties?

Professional socialization (which is also a de-socialization from one's previous life) mostly proceeds by way of self-instruction and informal exchanges. The content of this learning is neither open and verifiable nor conscious. These attitudes are integrated little by little. This part of the program is not voluntary: it is the tacit instructions that make each student into a self-taught graduate, whether it is in sport, art, informatics or whatever. In this way, amateur musicians, school pupils, sick people, all discuss and instruct each other in the solutions to shared problems. Such "learning by doing" is often passed over in silence and, in consequence, is unregulated. Becker recognizes that the adjustment to generally accepted norms take place by trial and error, by "playing" at being an average student, aiming, for example, at the middle of the class ranking and then observing the behavior of the others. (Donald Roy [1952] notes this in his observation of the assembly line workers that he worked alongside for a year.)

If Becker, like Roy in an industrial setting, concealed his second "profession," this was not a question of snobbery. "Playing" the piano in public keeps oneself up to date with the flow of social movements. It was Becker's way to resist being ground down and to sustain his curiosity about unexpected cultural realities. "Keep your hand in" – both literally and figuratively: that was his implicit message to the students for whom he would play the piano after their meetings. If they asked why, I assume that his reply would have been: "I am playing for you, after our discussion, not to display a virtuosity that separates us but to show you that theory is inseparable from practice, that a second craft in sociology is essential to succeed in the first – if only to avoid taking oneself too seriously." There is still a subliminal message: read between the lines and between the notes!

The Sociology of Professionals

Throughout his published work, Becker has insisted on his debts to Everett Hughes, and to his other contemporaries at the University of Chicago. The recent discovery of Becker's work in France allows us to grasp that this was a great collective enterprise in sociology (Chapoulie 2001). Its central theme was the study of professionals. This was not confined to members of the traditional professions – the thief is also an unacknowledged professional. The application of an external cri tique to a corporate institution – especially to a prestigious one – is a way to resist the stance that idealizes its activities because of the qualifications that it requires for membership (so that failures are attributed to chance or to *force majeure*). This was the program that was gradually established by the Chicago sociologists. They showed how the interests of service providers, especially those who held established positions, took precedence over the interests of their clients. The immediate goals of any organization were its own survival, through the protection of its members, the stabilization of their work, and the protection of working conditions that they considered acceptable. At the heart of professional actions were resistance to outside pressures, and to client influences. The antiquity of the profession was cited as a mark of its value, and its entitlement to legitimacy.

If the users of the profession's services were not entangled in a web of rules and practices that were rigged against them, their everyday judgments would create chaos, and destabilize the managed orderliness of the organization. The result would be anarchy. The double movement of professional careers, both horizontal and vertical, with stability as a priority, enacts this reality. The fate of new entrants is often that of job changes, adjustments to a new position, acceptance for tactical reasons that one's initial work will be unattractive – but that it can lead to better things. The internal pressures of the group to respect age and seniority, in exchange for learning from experience, constitute a gift relationship – gifts exchanged between the young and the old. The internal differentiation of work divides tasks at the same level into numerous informal grades, higher and lower, superior and inferior, although everyone is formally at the same stage of qualification.

Moral judgments, and the assessment of virtual mobility, are also constant features of lower-status work, but in a different sense. This is what Hughes described as "the social drama of work." It was Chicago sociology's central contribution to the inversion of traditional perspectives. Instead of taking the management perspective, they would take that of the workers or low-level employees. According to Donald Roy, management would tell the workers: "You are not working hard enough." The workers said to themselves: "it is not necessary to do more: go and screw yourself" (Roy 1952). The workers would decide among themselves how much work to deliver on an average day, a level that was, in their eyes, fair and consistent with preserving the quality of their workplace relationships, without disrupting them by excessive zeal or risking the speed-up of their work targets.

In place of a vision derived from the "natural" hierarchy of elites or employers, the Chicago School took that of tradesmen and subordinates. Their sociology reversed concerns about whether activities were or were not legal. You could, for example, think of theft in a general sense as a service industry, as some Chicago sociologists did. It facilitated the redistribution of wealth and reduced the tensions arising from social inequality. With the same impertinence, Everett Hughes showed that both prostitutes and priests, whether in bed or in the confessional, learned things about their clients that had to remain secret. As a result both trades demanded the same kind of deontology.

These statements were not obvious in 1950. They have become easier to accept now that we are consumers of interactions with the services that dominate the economy, and which are increasingly extending to shape the transformations of matter and nature in industry and agriculture. If you look hard enough, you will always discover a perspective on the activity that is more analytic, more enlightening than others. It advances our understanding of this interesting trade, stimulating those readers who only have a narrow or abstract vision. This is exactly what sociology is about: to make understanding simpler, to make the reader more intelligent and better informed. To make some bold analogies, consider how drug use is treated as a plague while, in contrast, alcoholism is tolerated as a domestic accident without serious consequences, protected by the relativity of moral judgments. The way in which the infractions of reputable, white collar, financiers or bank traders are tolerated can be contrasted with the severe penalties for workers who damage machines or commit petty thefts.

Nowadays we are more sensitized to the nature of transgressions and the relativity of the judgments that are made about them, of the modulations of the penal code between "excusable faults," on the one hand, and rigorous penalties, on the other. This is, in large part, thanks to sociology's development of *labeling theory*, the study of criminality and delinquency defined through the official categorizations of the police and the courts. To name something is to fix it and classify it according to the norms of a language: it is labeled. As we put it into words, we place it in a context or on a scale of value. Descriptions are never neutral – they always provide within themselves for an action. All of this has become obvious since the first publication of *Outsiders* in 1963.

The work of Becker and his predecessors has become common sense. We can no longer imagine the arguments that they had to go through to defend their position as well as the performances that were necessary to protect themselves against judicial accusations of inciting deviance. Because the attribution of breaches of work discipline, or professional conventions, also derives from established norms, the labeling approach by sociologists disturbed legislators, media columnists, lawyers, police and conservative opinion.[9] The description of cannabis smokers, depending upon whether they were termed users, consumers of soft drugs or addicts, opened a debate about who controlled the meaning, and who made judgments, and, therefore, who could legitimize or challenge the sanctions that were applied to them. Such labelling anticipated the emerging dilemma of the middle classes in evaluating the worth of services and the actions of their providers. While applying the same rules and terms to all consumers simplified the practice of classification, this created a moral challenge. One example of this problem: the identification of deviants as legitimate targets for the actions of social services, while rejecting their demands – for instance, for the supply of methadone to help overcome opiate addiction – define two contradictory poles of social intervention. The argument, "They are culpable in the eyes of the law but not responsible from an ethical point of view," has allowed a section of the middle classes to set themselves up as moral entrepreneurs. The professionals who intervene occupy a paradoxical position – caring for the deviants while simultaneously condemning them by reference to current norms of public health and well-being.

This sociology of professionals (Where do they come from? What do they do? What do they claim to be useful about their work?) leads Becker to judge sociology and its own practices. Each time the discipline addresses a problem, it wants to add something definite to the sum of its actions.

> The key to solving my problem, of connecting the almost philosophical approaches that are current in sociology with the collective activities that constitute a movement, has always been empirical work...My "difficulties" in this area of thought derive from my insistence on seeing concrete objects within the social situations where they are to be found, even though most

experts in the discipline habitually talk at the level of ideas, that is to say theoretically. I am always skeptical about sociological ideas that are not anchored in the reality of things, in the specific acts of specific people, in brief of ideas that are separated from flesh and blood individuals.

(Becker: Lecture at the Université de Grenoble, 2006).

The Sociologist as a Humble Laborer

The perspective or the dimension of the "sociologist as an ordinary worker," which Becker was the first to exploit ethnographically (Hughes, through his interactionist sociology, had showed him the way) implicitly presents us with the question: "Why do we have so many books about the sociology of work but so little application of sociology to the work of sociologists themselves?" Why are there so few studies of the sociologists' trade compared with the application of the sociology of work in the study of other scientists? Why is there so little sociology of sociologists? Professional shyness? The result of some kind of professional disorder or instability of judgment? Just as with introductory courses in medicine, we subtly instruct students in sociology about their collective responsibility, and the corporate strategies for defending the discipline. Professional etiquette demands that we avoid public criticism of a colleague or of the collective to which we belong. It is, for example, a fundamental principle of medicine that one should not draw the attention of legal authorities to a colleague who is considered dangerous, although this contradicts the ethics that are proclaimed to the public. This hidden discrepancy feeds off the respect for elders, for traditions (such as hazing) and demonstrates the solidarity of the profession, its deference to an accepted body of knowledge, and to the disciplinary rules. Becker's critique of the recruitment to the ranks of teachers leads him to remark that the profession of sociology avoids asking questions about teaching competence because it cannot respond with any consensus to the question of what should be taught.

Becker asks himself how teaching might be improved. If we read him properly, between the lines, he is promoting a parallel activity that would involve leaving the institution temporarily in order to do research full time. He reflects on a possible reconciliation between scientific research, which is difficult to evaluate for the human sciences (other than to accord the editorial boards of journals indisputable qualities of wisdom and judgment) with the mission of educating young recruits – particularly those in introductory classes – who are not the most receptive students. The teacher-researcher's difficulty in uniting these elements of their work deserves more consideration. Dangers arise from the rigor with which reports or theses are evaluated and the resulting obsession to conform to a standard that is both formalistic and dogmatic. What we usually teach students seems to fall like a word from heaven that is never made flesh. Becker offers a provisional solution to the problem. He does not hesitate to share with students his concerns about the fragility of his data, drawing attention to the contingencies that disrupted his initiatives or even led to their failure. At the same time as he is teaching, he is developing among the young a greater degree of clarity and balance in their reflections upon themselves. While spending hours in discussion with them in an office with an open door, he unsettles their own assumptions, their inevitable mistakes, and their ungrounded rhetoric. This approach contributes to the development of novices, who can discover the ambiguities, and the slipperiness, within the approaches taken by their teachers.

It is not easy to help a beginner. Each step depends upon others which, in effect, are shaped by an unspoken authority. The collection of materials is linked to a set of demands for credits and authorizations that limit the researcher's freedom of inquiry. The work of writing, as portrayed to the beginner, is more complicated in practice, particularly for those who do not come from an intellectual background and, quite reasonably, do not understand the conventions of publication (Which journal should an article be sent to? How should it be presented to the editor?). *Tricks of the Trade* (Becker 1998) was written to make such knowledge more accessible. Becker decided to lift the veil on some of the secrets learned by the members of the inner circle. It is best to identify one's readership at an early stage – dissertation adviser, other students or researchers, sponsors, readers of journals. Publication is a process with its own distinctive culture that must be learned through experience in dealing with its many uncertainties and negotiations with editors about changes and cuts. In the absence of consensus within the discipline, Becker, who has directed relatively few dissertations but been a member of a large number of committees, has committed himself not to press his demands beyond what might be reasonable. He supports young researchers by reassuring them about the inevitable outcomes of their trial and error. It may be better to pass someone who is less competent than to trash the career of a future innovator with a strong independent will. If I can judge from the juries where I have sat alongside him, he is uncomfortable in the role of an assessor who must make hard decisions.

The intergenerational exchange that he advocates by means of a mutual, and lightly selective, tolerance is also a form of professional reflexivity. He has developed this in many short pieces, as well as in books and articles, that point the finger at the conflicts and obstacles that are raised, not by a clumsy researcher, but by the uneasy and unstable history of the discipline of sociology. The work of sociology and the work of the sociologist are not the same thing. Much "sociology" is not carried out by credentialed sociologists. It is the discipline that acknowledges and sanctions an author, but there are many cases that lie beyond its reach. No sociologist has been able to define the collection of activities and obligations that would constitute a shared objective for sociologists. None of us even knows this intuitively because there are no hard definitions and the range of skills and applications is both infinite and infinitely variable.

In *Sociological Work* Becker (1970) responds in his own fashion to the question of the origins of sociology. He does not take this up at the highest level, through a universal definition in the name of the discipline's founding principles, synthesized in its traditions and still current. Nor does he take it up at the lowest level, that is to say by accepting total variability, complete indeterminacy as to whether any act or discourse might form part of the craft. He considers that his teachers at Chicago had taken an important step with their insistence on the empirical description of social groups. He attacks the problem, then, from the middle with the immediate objective of providing the greatest possible information to novices.

Through his major texts, initiating beginners and provoking reflections among his colleagues (*Writing for Social Scientists; Sociological Work; Tricks of the Trade*), Becker lays out resources and data on the craft of sociology. A knowledge of the everyday tasks involved in pursuing the trade, such as those of getting oneself known, recognized, and published, of getting favorable reports, developing professional self-respect, and meeting contractual obligations, is inescapable – so we should seek to grasp and analyze them. Every craft requires an apprenticeship. Socialization into the career track, contact with peers, hanging out with seniors, all introduce the individual to a professional culture. This introduction is the function of the organization, of pedagogic encounters, and of the acquisition of a social network. It has often been discussed how the experience of Chicago shaped an extended cohort of friends from 1950 until 1970. Their shared identity was epitomized by their mocking caricatures of the rival cohorts who studied with Lazarsfeld at Columbia or with Parsons at Harvard. Becker has just pressed this reflexivity further than his colleagues.

This shared and lived experience may seem somewhat nebulous compared with the strict standards set by the great universities of the East Coast of the United States. They were young people who were part of a vaguely formulated project running over several decades that no participant called the "Chicago School" at the time. They did not claim to be interactionists, ethnographers or qualitative sociologists but they developed a body of work that others identified as an interpretive community, as Chapoulie (2001) has documented.

In summary, the Chicago sociologists defined themselves in pragmatic terms through their enthusiasm for professional interactions and discussions between peers and colleagues. The portrait of the group is one of a social network. The members were relatively less individualistic than is common in universities, certainly less so than most of their colleagues. They applied an identical approach in studies of the commodities, images, ideas, books and property that threaded through their everyday lives. It is certain that this branch of American sociology has seized the "sociological imagination" to the point of devoting as many reflections and discussions to its work as to the rest of American sociology combined. It has been given a name, a stance, a degree of celebrity. This focuses on a set of ideas developed over three or four generations – 1920–1930; 1930–1950; 1960–1980 and still surviving: three generations of spiritual heirs, if you like. Becker is part of the third wave. This "co-operation" did not create a tightly knit and static collective, still less a cult, but a loose association of young scholars trained in the same fashion, which they shared among themselves in their thinking and their writing. Becker and his colleagues acknowledge each other to an unusual degree: at least twenty or so "accomplices" are thanked for their comments. The creation of sociological work in this fashion presents the appearance of a community. This is a paradox in an environment that focuses relentlessly on individual success and gives the greatest prominence to those who create the most divisions and quarrels. We can see the way in which this collaboration works in the collection *The Other Side* edited by Becker (1962).

The sociologists who shared the same education as Becker were shaped by the teachings of pragmatism, and by their reading of William James, which considered practice as a form of knowledge and empirical observation as a type of analysis. Their approach to causation is distinctive because they allow for the role of chance and indeterminacy in interaction. They were more sensitive to this mode of reasoning because of their own experiences as employees, low-paid workers before they received their degrees in sociology; working in low-level, temporary or casual jobs and, for some, the raw experience of war and the soldier's trade. Chance brought them to encounter in their studies a group of teachers who were not cut off from the world. They witnessed both contests and collaborations, even if competition and rivalry often led to splits: Everett Hughes and Lloyd Warner versus Herbert Blumer and Louis Wirth, for example (Abbott 1999). Students, though, were showered with encouragements to open themselves to the world, to join a living community ("Go get the seat of your pants dirty in real research," in Robert Park's famous phrase[10]).

Research into the mysteries of professions, from the most legitimate to the least honorable, formed part of their apprenticeship. Becker's close friend, Eliot Freidson, made a masterful study of medicine, revealing many secrets, attitudes and practices that were unknown to the lay public. He was challenged by the medical profession through its unions and its associations. This was a mark of the power of a profession that knew how to cover up the mistakes and failings of its members. Chicago sociology anticipated the explosive growth of power that was about to be detonated, throwing up a diversity of specialists, experts and communicators as successors to an industrial world of uniformity. The philosophy of experience that had its moment of glory at Chicago (from the presence of Dewey, Mead and Park) steered sociology toward testing itself in the confrontation with society rather than being content with the judgments of peers and selection panels. One outcome of their distinctive approach could be seen in the journal *Social Problems*, which Becker edited for a while. One could be simultaneously an interactionist and a Marxist, an interactionist and a historian or simply an ethnographer of problems, whether urban or everyday. *Outsiders* was the thread that led to this collective experience. It is a book that is widely cited, almost the subject of a cult. Its international success is partially due to the emergence of interactionism and its way of working, for which it is a kind of standard bearer. The scholars collected under this banner asked Becker to lead their formal association (*Society for the Study of Symbolic Interaction*). He refused but he has given this movement a substantial body of empirical work, which is lacking in some of the other manifestos for this group.[11]

Notes

1 *Outsiders* was first published in the US in 1963, and included reprints of papers published from 1953 onwards in US journals. It was not published in a French translation until 1985.

2 "Amateurs" here has also the sense of "fans" or enthusiasts, whose detailed knowledge and scholarship of a topic like jazz – or graphic novels or science fiction movies or whatever – makes a substantial contribution to understanding these fields that complements the work of a "professional" sociologist.

3 The *École Normale Supérieure* (ENS) is one of the "grandes écoles" at the pinnacle of the French system of higher education. Unlike French universities, they are relatively small institutions where entry is selective and highly competitive. Their graduates tend to dominate the private and public sectors of French society. Verdet (1997) describes her postgraduate experience in Chicago in a special issue of *Sociétés Contemporaines*. This published the contributions to a 1996 conference in France examining the legacy of Everett Hughes. Further biographical information on Verdet can be found (in English) at http://www.thedivinemercy.org/news/She-Transformed-Her-Grief-into-Acts-of-Love-6633 [accessed January 26, 2018].

4 This particular collection only exists in French. It translates most of Donald Roy's important contributions to industrial sociology from his ethnographic studies of workplaces. Later citations are to the originals where these can be identified.

5 The non-traditional recruitment was substantially aided by the Servicemen's Readjustment Act of 1944, also known as the G.I. Bill, to assist veterans returning to employment at the end of World War II. The provisions of this Act included scholarships for attending universities and colleges that opened access to many social groups that were previously excluded on financial grounds.

6 Robert Park (1864–1944) had previously worked as a journalist and as an assistant to the prominent African American scholar and activist, Booker T. Washington (1856–1915). He was a lecturer at the University of Chicago (1914–1923) before being appointed as a full professor. He retired in 1933, although he continued to be professionally active until his death in 1944.

7 Howard Becker suggests that the explanation is simpler: no one has thought that a translation would be commercially viable. On the other hand, the French medical profession is notoriously conservative. Jean Peneff is certainly right to draw attention to the offence that the analysis would cause if it were more accessible to French medical readers.

8 See Hughes et al. (1958).

9 Becker does not recall any such problems in the US. Peneff may be referring to the book's reception in France.

10 The full quote is: You have been told to go grubbing in the library, thereby accumulating a mass of notes and liberal coating of grime. You have been told to choose problems wherever you can find musty stacks of routine records based on trivial schedules prepared by tired bureaucrats and filled out by reluctant applicants for fussy do-gooders or indifferent clerks. This is called "getting your hands dirty in real research." Those who counsel you are wise and honorable; the reasons they offer are of great value. But one more thing is needful: first hand observation. Go and sit in the lounges of the luxury hotels and on the doorsteps of flophouses; sit on the Gold Coast settees and the slum shakedowns; sit in Orchestra Hall and in the Star and Garter burlesk [sic]. In short, gentlemen, go get the seat of your pants dirty in real research. This was recorded by Howard P. Becker (no relation) as a graduate student in Chicago during the 1920s and appears on p. 71 of J.C. McKinney, *Constructive Typology and Social Theory* (New York: Appleton-Century-Crofts, 1966). On Howard P. Becker, see http://howardsbecker.com/news_two_howies.html [accessed January 26, 2018].

11 Becker was the first editor of the Society's journal, *Symbolic Interaction*, in 1977–1978.

3

THE SOCIAL WORLDS OF ORGANIZATIONS, INSTITUTIONS AND PROFESSIONS

At the intermediate level of Becker's analysis, we find the concept of the "social world." He defined this in a discussion at Grenoble with Alan Pessin, in contrast to Bourdieu's concept of a "field" (Becker and Pessin 2017). The difference is not just a matter of the space that is invoked by the metaphor – three dimensions or two? It is a subtle distinction, but not an imaginary one. As Becker puts it: "I am not a great fan of reading Bourdieu. The sentences are too long and too convoluted to justify the benefit that one might get from them." Apart from the co-operation that is the necessary preliminary to all conflict, Becker distinguishes his approach from that of Bourdieu in this fashion: "In such a [social] world people do not respond automatically to mysterious external forces surrounding them" (Becker and Pessin 2017, p. 94).

This level, of interactions that are not determined, and therefore never complete, is inherently resistant to sociology's imperialist claims to understand it in terms of social systems or logics of power or whatever. Becker does not restrict the idea of domination to the outcome of competition or the struggle for status or economic resources. His concept of a "social world" is more open than one that is defined by constraints, restrictions on entry and relations of domination based on competition. He also sees acts of renunciation, of abandonment, of exit from the space, of willingness to take part and to collaborate with those who dominate it, of a desire to play with its rules. The social world is not an entity: this is why Becker always uses the metaphor in the plural. The monopoly of symbolic violence is, he says, never complete and never fixed. Interactions are complex and many-sided relationships in an open space where individuals continue to exercise a degree of freedom (to evade, to manipulate, to leave) within boundaries that are neither insurmountable nor eternal. At all times, "forces," "structures" and "dispositions" are weakened – who knows why? – but such events are constantly confirmed by the experience of history as the outcome of the actions of groups in the course of process. The results cannot be deduced *a priori* from the multitude of interacting movements.

Becker offers another example. As strong as a profession might be, it encounters obstacles in its practice and defines the legitimate ways of dealing with them. The profession tries to improve its work for its own benefit. For example, there are many limits to the expansion of medicine: technical, economic, political and scientific. Nevertheless, medicine maintains its moral authority thanks to a willing acceptance by the sick that can never be taken completely for granted. This may not be immediately obvious, because medicine presents a display of hierarchy and a forest of autonomous branches. The physicians set themselves up in specialties, whose accepted rules and practices vary according to the sectors within which they are applied. Every practitioner needs to take account of two hierarchies: the respect of their peers and seniors within their own specialty, and the recognition of the place of that specialty relative to others. Although medicine is officially a free profession, it is actually the focus of many strict and obscure regulations, with burgeoning legal implications that are more or less permanently under discussion. This is without any reference to the constraints that are initially learned by novices: respect for seniority, for established practitioners or masters of the craft, so that the spirit of authority that flows from their experience shapes diagnoses and clinical interventions. It is in this context that we see the function of medical education as achieving the submission of the young physicians: this is signaled by the provocative title, *Boys in White* (Becker et al. 1961), which so angered the profession.

Within the manifestations of Becker's "worlds," constraint is always recognizable: whether it concerns the limits of knowledge, the limits of the budget, the nature of the available equipment or the resistance of clients. A physician may not be able to carry out the examination that they would like to because of a lack of funds or admitting privileges at a hospital (especially today with the cost of tests and materials). Practice experience is developed within the constraints of budgets and the equipment available in laboratories. This is the situation for most of the things that go on within a profession or an organization. The premier competition between laboratories or test providers is for cash, which means serving the most affluent: legitimacy is based less on the results than on the satisfaction of the better-off. We can easily see that organizational constraints do not exist in a vacuum. They reflect an extraordinary variety of evolutionary pathways which only direct observation of experience will allow us to understand. How can we do this? What concepts might help us?

Rules or Conventions, Interactions or Coincidences?

The "subjects" of Becker's work are not individuals, agents or rational actors, neither are they obscure forces or mysterious structures. They are recognizable groups, concrete organizations, visible professions or identifiable institutions. Instead of explaining these in terms of systems, he sees a level of interactions, including empirical obstacles and constraints, that displays observable regularities. He uses the term "conventions" (habits, customs, standard operating procedures) to describe these. This label does not exclude random elements, strategies developed in small groups, chances and alternative possibilities, or dilemmas and contradictions. All these exist in the life of such collectivities, although not in an infinite variety. They are all examined in the same fashion, underlining the threads woven by the individuals who are linked to a situation, to the achievement of a shared reality. This is why, in every collectivity that comes together regularly to pursue a definite goal, the researcher will find explicit or tacit regulations, the rules of living that are indispensable to the coordination of shared tasks. Even if the rules within the group are not strictly defined, the group operates within an external framework (statutes, judicial decisions, formalized rituals). There is a legal and political context to every action, from the simplest governance of smoking or playing jazz on Sundays to the most complex acts of repression. This context is realized through the means of prohibitions and tolerances, the application of legal norms, of deals and of silences.

Having said that, Becker also makes an obvious and sensible point. The "laws" that regulate our collective life, by classifying acts on a principled basis, cannot cover all possibilities, particularly those that were not clearly envisaged at the time they were created. Given the evolution of the specified acts and the techniques that produce or sustain them (a new smoking product or an old one that has been chemically modified, for example), every law or explicit norm provokes an opposite reaction. There is an immediate desire to resist or evade the law, because a social group is impacted by it. The channels of distribution and consumption are adapted and parallel resources evolve to facilitate the rule-breaking. Any rule, even if it is not rigid and bearing heavily on those affected, generates, at the very least, inconsistencies in its application, deviations in practice or strategies for its manipulation. We are all surrounded by rules, straitjacketed by innumerable regulations of which we know little, let alone be able to turn to our advantage. No rule can anticipate all the difficulties in applying it: we cannot anticipate every possible case and new cases are always appearing. There is always "deviance," even of the most anodyne kind (like crossing the street outside the marked crosswalk). If a law exists, there is inevitably disobedience and deviance.

However, we should never neglect the role of chance in the chaos of social life. Many events are accidental. As a result, then, Becker stresses that we should not concentrate too much on the officially proclaimed norms and working principles (moral precepts, codes of conduct, formal regulations). He replaces this heap of rigid laws that have fallen into disuse by what he calls conventions: habitual actions that stabilize the meaning of a rule or work around it in order to make faster progress, to get a better deal for oneself or to bring a wider benefit to everyone. From this, he defines two different senses of the term "convention":

(a) The traditional meaning. A customary practice, a flexible way to get around difficulties, to devise an exit from a dead-end. As so often in his writings, Becker is not very explicit about the substance of his ideas. He is a pragmatist: nevertheless, we can infer his meaning from the examples he gives, of activities and the new situations that they generate. Conventions are a way to live "economically" in society without having to explain the motivations for all of our acts and the resources that they draw on. Conventions are what allow us to develop routines that are the basis of a stable social order, despite all the difficulties that arise in the course of developing shared actions. The auto-pilot that makes survival possible creates a limited number of conventions. Every society develops its own stock responses, despite the contingencies that arise every day: for example, there are conventions that suspend the rules of orthography (in text or SMS messages), of grammar (in telegrams), of politeness in emergency situations or for the purpose of adapting to new media (the internet and information technologies). Such conventions can sometimes become so frequent that they are transformed into habits: no one really notices that they are being used and applied in a more or less mechanical fashion.

The rapidly changing contingencies of our shared existence lead us to push back against any rigid form of organization. A great space of freedom is opened for those who know how to take advantage of it. Everyone knows how to do this, or can, at least, guess. Otherwise society could not function. Of course, like Durkheim, Becker believes in rules, in fixed points, official frames, but he does not over-estimate their impact because he is also capable of seeing the contrary elements, the impossibility of a social order that is completely regulated and subject to arbitrary power. Sociology should hold to a degree of modesty and prudence when it claims to be able to publish categorical "results" let alone to talk of "laws"!

(b) The second sense may seem to be less important. This refers to the occasional adaptations of the main usage to introduce some flexibility with minimal effort on specific occasions when something unexpected or unknown happens. For a motorist, the signal from the lights of another, oncoming, driver may mean several things: watch out for a hazard (an unexpected obstacle in the road; a car stopped on the highway) or the presence of police officers or a radar trap. The initial objective is one of safety, a collective warning, sharing information or immediate gain if the collusion helps to avoid a traffic fine by announcing a police ambush. Such conventions are not illegal: they are tolerated rather than totally illegitimate, although they can be both at the same time. The code of the road is made up of principles for specific actions that are the craft of driving one's vehicle correctly (the driving test allows one to believe that everything is predictable). These have developed as a basis for the fundamental knowledge that everyone needs to acquire in order to drive easily and safely. Social life is like a highway that is jammed with very different kinds of vehicles, from pedestrians to cyclists, from horses to Ferraris. As we all know, though, when the traffic lights are not working at an intersection or there is no traffic police officer when an unexpected obstacle appears, the result is not necessarily the anarchy of a traffic jam where everyone risks being held up. In practice, the road users wanting to reach their destination suspend the code on their own initiative and adapt to the new situation. A temporary convention among the users comes into operation (although it may evolve and adapt), just as with the reactions of any crowd in publicly welcoming a novel product or a new art form. In that moment, the cultural code is suspended and people make signs that are not in any manual of taste. There is an agreement between the participants that former usages will be discarded: priority will be given to this new definition of the situation in order to clear a way forward.

For progress to occur in any society, it is essential not to be bound by the letter of the rules when the norms do not foresee the results that are occurring. In dealing with a situation that the laws did not envisage, people may decide to ignore them, at least for that time and place, and improvise an order that is more useful in that moment. Societies need such conventions which provide fuzzy and temporary rules that enable progress to continue when the route ahead is unexpectedly blocked. In other contexts, the rules of grammar and orthography are often suspended or inverted by linguistic innovations that become conventions among specific social groups: backslang[1] or other word games where a sentence means the exact opposite or is undercut by its intonation. Social life is built on such indispensable adjustments which are deplored only by purists in jurisprudence or grammar. Nevertheless, laws that are poorly adapted to current situations, or practices that have fallen into disuse, continue to be present. Any implicit agreement to work around them comes with some risks. This attitude can become second nature – setting aside moral obligations without making oneself accountable to them. The suspension or abolition of definitions of deviance signify rapid changes in the substance of social control in the face of upheavals among its consumers.

Shifts in opinion and a necessary evolution of toleration for "what is happening anyway" can be made to happen by small independent groups, or by the society as a whole, so that people can better continue to pursue their collective interests (this is not a "general" interest, which is a loaded term) even if a secondary objective is to maintain a practical hierarchy and a working consensus. Becker has turned his uncommitted perspective on many of the social processes that avoid permanent negotiation in dealing with unusual events or serious problems. If societies were marked by a logic of obedience to all power, and internalized docility, there would be no judges, lawyers or police officers, and no need for numerous regulatory frameworks. Many practices in the work of industry, medicine or commerce, opened up by this sociology of erratic decision-making, are the residue of events that re-emerge in every generation. For all their power and authority, great institutions still find them hard to track and co-ordinate.

The Major Institutions and Their Constraints

How can we understand institutions, whether as a beginner or as a lay person? This level of analysis is Becker's "social world." A complex institution develops according to its own temporal rhythms because of its multiple functions, the flexibility with which its roles are interpreted, and the slow diffusion of change. Its primary function is to endure, which is regularly described as "institutional inertia." The reflex of any organism is to seek to survive periods of danger or austerity, at least as far as its employees or agents are concerned. The persistence of apparently useless practices shows us the nature of this resistance. We can see how avant-garde or other "revolutionary" groups take hold of established codes, or traditional justifications, for an institution, with the intention of abolishing them and replacing them by others: a commonplace of dialectical reasoning. In doing so, however, these practices are re-energized with the result that the revolution has contributed something to their persistence. No society can ever wipe the slate completely clean.

When it is necessary to adapt, though, the institution often goes on doing what it was already doing while proclaiming that it has changed, often in a rather random fashion. The idea of a "social lottery,"[2] one of Becker's main concepts, only seems to be paradoxical. The inevitability of rule-breaking, the apparently endless nature of action, the unforeseeability of outcomes appear to be determined. At the same time, we see a plethora of missing actions, failed adaptations, situational misunderstandings, twisted intentions, perverse effects, and even counter-productive strategies. Such transgressions are assessed as either beneficial or damaging from the perspectives of the various actors, whether judges or judged. In my view, this is why Becker, who initially focused on the phenomenon of deviance by officials found himself, perhaps involuntarily, in the position of a dissident theorist. He directly confronts the logic of determinism by recognizing circumstance, chance and fortune as counterweights to the intense effects of social relationships and the multiplicity of possible causal explanations.

At the biggest scale of "social worlds," large collectivities of people in organizations supported by states with explicit structures, their complexity demands concepts that have been little used until now by empirical researchers. We need to draw on social history and comparative studies to examine established organizations that may be hundreds of years old, whose actions are slow and gradual, whose existence is shaped by processes at the level of nations or continents. An institution cannot be reduced to its officially proclaimed functions: that would assume a design or purpose that should be the topic of sociological inquiry. For example, the family is a great institution that begins the socialization of children, shares food, and is a primary source of social and emotional support. The school is another resourceful and multi-faceted institution that cuts across society. It does more than transmit knowledge. Teaching involves instruction, moral development, education, developing critical faculties, diffusing aesthetic tastes and customary ways of thinking, and acting or interacting. Schools provide entry to all sorts of domains: science, religion, civil society, art, and sport. Nevertheless, the development of our human capacities does not take place exclusively in schools, but also in other places of initiation, from the most legal to the most illicit. Self-development is learning to live in a different way as much as a preparation to enter the world of work.

In the same historical context, the project of medicine has become much wider than the simple action or intention of "caring." Art is more than the aesthetic pleasure that it gives to our senses or the moral satisfaction that it brings to its creators. This term has become a very ambiguous shorthand because one finds art everywhere: the culinary arts; the art of conversation; the cave art of our ancestors; the art of primitive tools or household utensils. A stone worked by a prehistoric tool-maker would have had an aesthetic value for its users that is quite different from those who contemplate it in a contemporary exhibition. Everything that is symbolic (and it is rare that human activities do not have a symbolic element) acquires an aesthetic dimension from the pleasure of looking at it, of touching it or of talking about it. This is the source of the confusion. We find art everywhere: in architecture, in urban planning, in the construction of furniture, in household design, in the presentation of food, in the planting of gardens, in clothing – and in conversation, in telling the story of an event or making a joke at the bar of a café (what we call "folk art").

Conventions are particularly numerous among the members of the most prestigious professions, whether or not these are bound to their traditions and their past history: the liberal arts, education, medicine, science. Art worlds are the outstanding example of those institutions that rest on tacit and unwritten conventions. The satisfaction of clients is only one perspective, one aspect of the power to define the criteria of beauty, taste and aesthetic perfection. In the production of art works, there are mysterious elements that shape the definition: the manufacture of the materials; the invention of techniques; the available musical instruments; the composition of paints; the means of reproduction and printing.

Art cannot be dissociated from the means by which it is diffused among those who are trained to recognize it. A song made by a single person, without an audience, however beautiful or harmonious it might be, is not a work of art. It must be grafted onto recordings, purchases, sales, exchanges – a whole series of activities that appropriate it for private or public consumption. Today, the bidders at auctions, the collectors, the gallery owners, the promoters of concerts, and the directors of museums seem to be unavoidable, without forgetting the role of patrons or the commissioners of public art. From the perspective of the market, art has created a business in commentaries from experts, in edited collections, and in public meetings of aesthetes.

The art market is shaped by the participation of users with different functions and interests. In order to understand these dimensions, such powerful forces, the sociologist must be armed with patience. How can this be done? If we look at the level of organizational analysis, Becker has, in the course of his career, studied the social worlds of urban elementary schools (his doctoral thesis), of a medical school (with Hughes and others), several art studios and rock concerts, topics in the arts selected for their level of complexity. In ethnography, we normally prefer to study relatively small groups, a few tens of people in a studio, a team, an orchestra, an aesthetic movement: or, in contrast, one can attack the problem at the level of the superstructure, the level of very general phenomena, of long-lasting groups. We rarely set out, as Becker does, to examine the middle level: the microscope is rarely turned on the intermediate structures, where he excels, those of groups of hundreds of individuals scattered between the summit and the base.

The Socio-historical Dimension

Unlike the concept of organization applied to an enterprise or an establishment, the functions of an "organized social world" are not easy to define in terms of a single dimension or a single space. A social world may bring together a hundred different trades, a great variety of knowledges, whether diffused or recognized, a national territory of operation. Since art worlds are a sometimes baroque assembly of very different institutions or, better, a bizarre galaxy of overlapping functions, they create, in their operation, networks of loose and intense relationships.

Historians of society customarily produce studies of relationships between worlds that are abstract and unbounded: regions, classes, nations. They deal with Big History, that of social movements, global alliances, on the scale of Revolutions and Reactions, economic crises and great wars. The idea that an interactionist history could see the light of day in France is still embryonic. In intellectual competition with Bourdieu, it is difficult for any discipline, however well-established, to promote such an approach. As a result, French sociology has missed its rendezvous with the methods of History, just as much as history has missed out on the methods of Sociology. Alain Touraine, whose original qualification[3] was in history, could have been an intermediary, but he lacked the courage of his convictions, received little encouragement from his mentor, Georges Friedmann, and has not left any legacy. History, however, has annexed – without acknowledgment – an "interactionist" orientation from the sociologists. We could note the work of contemporary American historians like the interdisciplinary studies of China from the "Irvine School" in California or the British comparative social anthropologists like Jack Goody.

Can this model of loosely articulated social worlds be applied to the production of material objects as much as to education, whose practices are protected by the autonomy of teachers within their classrooms?[4] Their uncertainties, the fluctuations of demand and supply, undermine the speculative projections of the planners. Two major books give an affirmative answer. They exemplify the interactionist approach to institutions proposed by Becker. *Les Collèges du Peuple* by Jean-Pierre Briand and Jean-Michel Chapoulie (1992) is an incursion by sociologists into territory that is usually the province of historians. It is justified by the lack of studies concerned with elementary schools: the study of higher levels of education has become widespread, particularly since the publication of *Les Héritiers* (Bourdieu and Passeron 1964). *Les Collèges* has inspired work by Christophe Andréo, Christophe Brochier, Phillipe Masson, Marc Suteau and others.

Another project, although apparently quite different, mixes scales and methods of research. This is *Les gens d'usine, 50 ans d'histoire à Peugeot–Sochaux* by Nicolas Hatzfeld (2002). These two substantial projects introduced a different way to use the methods of ethnography in historical studies by taking account of the medium term, a half century rather than a *longue durée*. [5]

In this ethno-history, the question of sampling does not arise as it does in the physical sciences. The theory of random sampling is a fallacy when applied to sociology, as Becker shows in *Tricks of the Trade* in what he calls synecdoche (Becker 1998, pp. 67–68).[6] Briand and Chapoulie (1992) set out the basic features of this kind of approach. The interactionist approach to institutions leads them to select a series of cases as representative of the spread of elementary education in

France from 1890 until World War II. The cases are parts that stand for the whole. The adoption of this ethnographic methodology in *Les Collèges* leads naturally to the use of Becker's concepts: the effects of power and organizational inertia, careers, local organization, trajectories, informal apprenticeship, the involvement with clients (in this case families). They conclude that the idea of a "single education" is misplaced.[7] There is not one model school, but several forms and types of schooling within the same framework. There is not a single politics of education but numerous simultaneous politics that are often discordant, and even contradictory. At the very least, they have invalidated the idea of "the school" in an abstract sense or of a general model of schooling.

The manufacture of automobiles is also a social world of its own, much like that of the art world. The production lines studied by Hatzfeld (2002) demonstrate this. Who does what to an automobile? Each stage has many facets: the lines, the various support departments, the different production sites – now often on different continents. All these converge on a single object – the automobile. The engine, the body with its lines of steel, electricity, plastic, its dashboard, its passenger compartment, the tires (which belong to another production process), the chassis, the hydraulic or electrical circuits, as well as the design and the degree of comfort, depend on different components which need to be integrated. But that is not all: other organizations intervene. There are the planners, the forecasters and the testers; then the sales teams and the exhibition services; marketing; publicity as well as delivery and recovery services. These multiply the interactions between technical and business departments that are necessary to get the automobile to the buyer's home. There are internal and external collaborations, interweaving lines of work: there is no better way to describe this than as "organizational interaction" to capture the tacit relations between the different elements of the production process. Becker understands art worlds in a similar fashion, where the work consists of interweaving the output of many individual producers. In the contemporary world, all manufacturing is complex: we should adopt this concept of the immensity of the "social world" as something that can be inferred, is concrete, and is not reducible to a vague and fuzzy group.

This is why it is better to analyze situations and interactions than to look for internalized "dispositions" that assume a mechanical form of determinism. Not every habit becomes a deeply rooted attitude. Variables such as social background, occupational status, level of education or schooling, or socio-economic experiences are means of simplifying analyses. These mark the differences in Becker's approach, through his silences. When he describes institutions or professions, he does engage in abstractions (stability, inertia, chance, situation) but he locates these in the circumstances where decisions are made, where there are forks in the road, where there are moments of mobility, horizontal or vertical, that elude the rational decision models of strategic plans or political actors. The idea of strategy, of a life spent in one of the major professions, provides him with an example of how such cases can be treated ethnographically. When he considers that no profession is so unified and co-ordinated as to solve all its internal problems, he infers that one cannot identify in advance the opportunity to gain access, to decide on methods of investigation, to be asked in desperation to bring order to overly complex training requirements. As a researcher, Becker targets his object at neither too high nor too low a level until he has a sufficient volume of substantial data. He has demonstrated this approach across a "sample" of four professions: physicians, physiologists, philosophers and engineers (Becker 1970, pp. 189–201).

All these studies carry out their comparisons by a process of abduction. Abduction can be contrasted with induction (reasoning from the base upwards) and deduction (reasoning from the top downwards). It is an approach developed by William James and John Dewey, which is distinguished from hypothetico-deductive reasoning by breaking down a series of somewhat comparable cases. It envisages a partial degree of causality derived from looking in parallel at a number of different cases, although not so many that they come to form a mosaic or a photo-montage. The art lies in marrying unexpected opposites. This methodology focuses on levels situated between ethnography and great socio-historical visions. It is Becker's preferred level of analysis. His book, *Telling About Society* (Becker 2007a) is an excellent example – it is a dictionary of surprising cases that finally prove illuminating.

Identifying the Critical Interactions

In sociology, our studies are constantly torn between research on groups at an ethnographic scale and on aggregates of individuals scattered through large structures. Historians are comfortable with their own tradition: studies of the past accept this division and move freely across it.

This is more difficult for the ethnographer. How can we recognize, in the middle of a multitude of interactions, those that are critical for explaining at that specific moment, what one can "see" or merely infer? The interactions entangle a first order of observations (the actors and their tasks) with a second order, of teams, local politics and general classifications of work. The articulation of these levels demands a refined knowledge of the interior of each target sector. Becker has given us a model. To be a player of a musical instrument or a connoisseur of artistic techniques (the piano, photography, the theatre) it is necessary, at the very least, to grasp their history, to overcome the challenges of entering into their milieu, of joining in collective productions, of finding a place in the organization of roles. But it is also necessary to access, at the highest level, the tacit knowledge that is often hidden by institutions whose official functions are to recruit, to sanction and to exclude.

In any area of work, then, the first question is this: what is the collectivity that holds the power to define the norms of operation and their results in everyday practice? This interweaving of levels of study cannot be defined in advance. This is why Becker underlines the risks of all premature definitions. The subject of a thesis or a research project emerges progressively. At the beginning, one does not necessarily have a clear view of where one is going. The direction becomes apparent as the investigation goes along. Arbitrary divisions into the "sociology of education," the "sociology of the arts," the "sociology of the professions" are of limited value. They may help in launching a project, but this soon departs from its initial thinking as the limits of its operational relevance become clear. The consequence is that ethnographers carry out studies at an intermediate level of sampling. *What is a Case?* (Ragin and Becker 1992) is a good example of the way to handle multiple cases.

In examining a planet, the astrophysicist does not use the same instruments, or carry out the same investigations, as a mathematician calculating infinity. We have the same problems as the observers of celestial bodies given the scale of our "specimen": societies in flux are as poorly understood as the cosmos. Becker deals with both dimensions by refocusing his spy-glass. It is easy to overlook this because he does not insist on it or describe clearly the movements of his operating practice, which just seem obvious to him.

Credibility is a Source of Power

This is another of Becker's great ideas. Becker mobilizes a formidable historical knowledge of culture to judge the credibility of evaluations and artistic judgments. This rests on several hundred works, mostly from outside sociology, reflecting the personal experiences of their authors. Each study serves to make more relative, more historically diverse, not artistic taste (undefinable), nor even the aesthetics of perceptions and emotions (personal and ephemeral), but the workings of the organizations of production. It is consistent with the idea that "art," both independent and officially approved, appears in a society in response to the conditions of the market. What is labelled as "art" in a society, sustaining, and paying for, an enterprise called "artistic production"? How do institutions disseminate this idea? Through education, through the definition of "fine arts," through museums and galleries, through establishments and monuments, through universities – all of which may confer or contest the label. The conflicts between social movements and rival theories of art bring this huge "apparatus" to life, filling the stage with eternal topics such as the meaning of a work, the definition of popular culture (cinema, television, pop music) or the role of "genius."

Material production requires the mobilization of means that spread far from the point of creation. There is a whole satellite world that clusters around the supporting cast: the assistants, the critics, the editors, the sales staff, the advertisers. Another essential circle brings together the collectors, the merchants and the whole reserve army of amateurs, who may or may not want to come on board for the career or to imitate it from near or far. The first constraint is the intangible nature of the content. What is art? Is what I am doing "art"? Where does art begin and end? The people who make copies of a canvas are not artists. We can paint like Cezanne, but this does not make us Cezanne but a duplicator or a plagiarist. A perfect copy receives no special recognition: we talk of reproduction or duplication, if not of duplicity. By definition, art challenges and changes the conventions of every epoch. The artist must invent, innovate, hustle, change the rules and manners of seeing or hearing. The sociology of the professionalization of art has suggested that "critical opinion" is always being reworked by the professionals who judge and class themselves as "creators" and argue about interesting positions.

In the same way with schooling, the trust and credibility of the users (parents) rests on years of shared experience and a multiplicity of entrenched regulations. The regulatory aspect is established as normative because of the danger, as far as the administration is concerned, of improvisation by their agents, such as the uncontrollable freedom of teachers in their classrooms. Beginning a study with a focus on this contradiction is a good point of entry into the substance of a profession that has both formal (the curriculum) and informal (the choice of pedagogy, the limits on personal initiatives) elements of control. But, above all, it is the financial resources that affect the different distribution of places for pupils, teaching spaces, staff, and working conditions. When Becker began his study of elementary school teachers, he saw that the intervention of parents would be the most important constraint because of the coexistence of different social classes in the public schools.

In their study of a medical school, Becker and his co-authors identified another constraint. The kind of life that the medical students lived within the school was then in the process of change. The dean and the administration were tolerating much more freedom on the campus, a style of student life in keeping with the spirit of the time, while maintaining their traditional prohibitions on challenging the modes of instruction. In a profession as elitist and as hierarchical as medicine these had not changed much for fifty years, although the control had become less obvious. The students were free in all respects except for the management of their workload, a domain reserved for their professors and the administration. This organizational constraint put great pressure on the space for student autonomy, where they were also supposed to learn how to get by in their future dealings with disease. Similar but less powerful constraints could be found in other disciplines – humanities, arts and communication being less prescriptive than law or economics. The instructional constraints imposed themselves through the annual examinations, the anonymity of the lecture theatre, the module requirements and the one-to-one tutorials, teaching methods that were more than five hundred years old and were not easily going to be changed.

While they are at university, students are coerced – more than they are aware – by the invisible organization. They have a calendar that is different from that of the lay world, the periods of vacation and the hours of classes. There are other restrictions: the budget, the particular interests of the professors that have been hired and their level of experience and seniority. The students encounter two types of authority: one that is written, although rarely evident, by the administration; and one that is more obvious and striking from their teachers. The selection at entry and the distribution of courses of study are aspects of the organization in the creation of student places. The power of the teachers only exists because the administration can ensure that the examinations are organized according to the traditional criteria – individualized assessment and grading. In deference to the faculty, the administration has little interest in student absenteeism or the content of the courses but is concerned with the ethics of students' behavior, as well as the legalities of awarding, or withholding, a degree – and protecting that decision from challenges in court.

The Politics of Chicago Sociology

Despite the work of Jean-Michel Chapoulie (2001), earlier studies by Yves Grafmeyer and Isaac Joseph (1979), and more recent ones by Suzie Guth (2000) and by Daniel Céfaï (2003), in addition to fifteen or so introductions to published works, there are still grey areas in understanding the Chicago School. The widespread criticism of US sociology, for a lack of militancy or commitment to liberal values, depends on the critics' view of "politicization," as distinct from an interest in political issues. The Chicago sociologists concerned themselves with groups that occupied a particular space and the definition of norms within this. Who acts and how? With whom and against whom? How are conflicts and agreements conducted? They carried out this program in a way that is unfamiliar to the politicized sociologist, to the point where they were assumed to be working in an intuitive fashion, producing brilliant descriptions of, for example, minority groups or processes of discrimination, without going any further. However, their analysis of different levels, from the most ethnographic to the most abstract or conceptual, reveals a different meaning to the term "politics." For example, within the framework of the established legal norms that define deviance, the debate between citizens and agents of social control takes on an additional level of understanding, turning back on the authorities who identify and sanction the deviants (for example, the users of prohibited drugs). Without taking sides or promoting conflicts, this information throws a new light on political actions. When they expose symbolic crusades – as Joseph Gusfield (1963) did – they are questioning the validity of a political stance. They open the possibility of a sociology of symbolic competition between the creators and promoters of different ideologies, advancing tolerance or repression. It is their way of being practical and useful to society, although less "red" as one might say.[8] As he dissects the social worlds of art or medicine, two bureaucratic monsters, Becker invites us to reflect on how everyday opinions are shaped, which is different from believing that one can influence trade unions or political parties.

In this sense, Becker and his colleagues are certainly "political" but it is not the gesture politics of the self-styled "engaged sociologists." The most conclusive demonstration of this "politicization" indubitably lies in the way Becker and his colleagues have been attacked for their studies of the most powerful social institutions: the police, the legal system, the medical profession. Becker himself says:

> The last formulation reminds us of the important role that power plays in interactionist theories of deviance (Horowitz and Liebowitz 1968). Under what circumstances do we make and enforce ex post facto rules? I think

empirical investigation will show that it occurs when one party to a relationship is disproportionately powerful so that he can enforce his will over others' objections, but wishes to maintain an appearance of justice and rationality. This characteristically occurs in the relations of parents and children and in the equally paternalistic compromise between social workers and their clients or between teachers and their students.

(Becker 2008, pp. 188–189)

Notes

1   "Le verlan" is a form of French slang based on the inversion of syllables in a word. For example, "femme" (woman) becomes "meuf."

2   "Hasard social." The translation is not a term that I can locate in Becker's work, but Peneff is drawing attention to Becker's frequent references to the unpredictability of social life, the elements of randomness that are captured in his use of terms like chance, fate, and opportunity. It reflects the French adoption of Becker's work to criticize the determinism of both Marxist and positivist currents in their sociology.

3   "Agrégation." This is a competitive examination for graduates planning to teach at the highest levels in the French educational system. It is divided into sections by discipline. Sociology has never had its own section, although it has formed part of one for "economic and social sciences" since 1977. Prior to this, most sociologists took the examination in philosophy, but Touraine had passed the examination in history. In practice, appointment as a full professor in sociology now tends to come from a pool of candidates who have obtained the "*habilitation à diriger des recherches* (HDR)." This is a higher level research degree beyond the PhD, involving another substantial thesis and an oral defense in front of a jury of established scholars.

4   Teachers in France retain much more autonomy in their pedagogy than would now be the case in England and some parts of the US.

5   The idea of the "*longue durée*" (literally "long duration") is associated particularly with the *Annales* School of French historians. They argued for the study of fundamental social, economic and cultural processes as determinants of historical developments over several centuries. Internationally, the best-known members are probably Fernand Braudel (1902–1985) and Emmanuel Le Roy Ladurie (1929-).

6   "Synecdoche" is a rhetorical term that refers to the use of a part of something to refer to the whole. Becker gives the example of the way in which "The White House" comes to stand not just for a building but for the whole institutional apparatus of the US presidency.

7   The reference here is to the cultural importance in France of the notion of education as a uniform, secular, experience through the state school system. Even where students attend private schools, these must follow the state curriculum in order to receive public subsidies that cover the costs of teachers' salaries. These schools tend to be affiliated with the Catholic Church and their status allows them to provide religious instruction within school hours, which is prohibited in state schools. Children are expected to attend their neighborhood school which means, in practice, that their educational experience can vary considerably more than the official description acknowledges.

8   US readers should note that "red" is the color of the left and "blue" the color of the right in most European countries. This inverts the association of the colors with Republican and Democrat parties in the United States.

4

FROM PRAGMATISM TO INTERACTIONISM

When we declare ourselves to be interactionists, we are choosing an intermediate level of analysis. But we still need to specify this level in more detail:

a   We might mean the study of small groups of individuals through ethnography. This uses observation, in all its forms, to understand the shifts in the relations between members that occur as a group reorganizes to confront new situations. Every group is doing this all the time in search of stability. Turbulence may arise from the evolutionary pressures of the times or from more intimate processes – in the family, the workplace or the local environment. The isolated individual does not exist. There is no *homo sociologicus*, a lifeless abstraction of little value.[1] "Individuals" and "group members" are the same thing. This conceptual amalgamation is not a source of confusion: it is fundamental to the interactionist approach.

b   We might mean the level of large independent organizations, where the sources of observational data are to be found in their archives, their internal documents, their inventories and staff records, and their accounts. Becker seldom refers to this more general level of social history. There is, however, a space, between total structural determinism and rational individualism, where we find institutions and individuals living in groups (families, workgroups, neighbors, localities, homesteads...). We could call this kind of analysis, the pragmatism of scale.

The approach to philosophy known as pragmatism is beginning to become known in France and elsewhere in Europe. Broadly speaking, American pragmatism is a branch of Anglo-Saxon philosophy which is interested in questions of aesthetics, of popular culture and of music. Becker has immersed himself in this tradition, without much citing it, since his days as a student: Chicago was a center for its diffusion, if not for its development (thanks to the influence of its professors, Mead and Dewey). This approach emphasizes the importance of "seeing" actions as they happen, of attention to praxis. Specifically, it is always the study of action. Who does what – and how do they do it?

Evolution, Process, Transformation

Society is constantly in a state of flux. Life in societies is continuous disruption, a more or less rapid or slow evolution. Our objective is to describe the adaptations that we call "process." This approach neither presumes nor determines the future. In this, it differs from theories such as those of individualism (methodological individualism or action theory), structuralism or functionalism, which assume they can identify emerging directions. They can then claim to speak in terms of changes they believe they can predict and describe. Becker has never claimed to be able to do this. He puts this quite simply:

> If you study collective action, you cannot avoid the knowledge that every-thing – every person, every group, every action, every event – has a history. Nothing just pops into existence in some mysterious way we must not inquire into. Things get the way they are over some period of time, and to think this way leads inevitably to a conception of process....Likewise, you cannot avoid the knowledge that events are transactional or interactional, that you understand what one person does by knowing the network of interaction he operates in and what all those other people are doing and how that conditions and is conditioned by what he does...To recommend that we study process and focus on interaction hardly seems revolutionary. I have tried in my own work to take those ideas seriously, accepting and following through on their implications even when that requires doing violence to accepted notions of how the world is or how sociologists out to study it. I am a naturalist...
>
> *(Becker 1970, p. vi)*

Becker sees the passage of time as the primary topic for research: time changes the phenomena that we describe. Organizations are always in an incomplete state of transformation – career paths branch, for individuals and the collective, and chains of events unroll. He elaborated, in a way that has become celebrated, the concept of "Becoming," the "emergence of the future," through his attention to transfor-mations of the self that came out of unacknowledged experiences: the passage from student to physician, from pupil to teacher, from non-smoker to smoker, from Sunday musician to professional, from hobbyist to specialist. Socialization into a new milieu occurs in time and space as much as in the context of the models that surround the process. Moreover, Becker immediately acknowledges the fluidity and the relativity of his "theories." In an interview where he discusses these limits, he readily accepts the criticism of his detractors.

My friends tell me that I do not understand the necessity of a historical approach and that I am not sensitive to the historical circumstances that have produced the fields that I have written about. I do understand what they are saying. I even agree with them. However, as a matter of temperament, education and a degree of laziness, I am not inclined to do anything about it. To tell you the truth, I am mostly uncomfortable with taking on the role of an intellectual, of being the kind of mentor that people sometimes want me to be. I can't take seriously all that stuff about sociology, the academic profession, the competition for prestige or ranking.

(Diani 1987, p. 40)

This is not just an elegant way of avoiding the question but an admission of powerlessness in the moment that is applicable to our whole profession. We can also acknowledge that, when he is criticized, he does not assert any right to reply because he does not claim to be the author of a doctrine, still less to offer a definitive statement. Becker's "system" is so little fixed that he himself is constantly revising it. He deploys an amused skepticism in the face of mysterious phenomena (the internalization of constraints or the creation of regularities) and of their miraculously effective application. It is a demonstration of the pragmatism that he learned at university.

All Research Is Limited By Time

Becker insists that the phenomena of classification and the imposition of educational standards never have immediate effects. They take time to manifest themselves. The legal practices involved in accusing someone of deviance, and the subsequent sanctions, similarly constitute a process with delayed consequences. Any interaction, however simple it may seem to be, unfolds in time with pauses, moments of strength and weakness, an irregular duration (from a few hours to several months) from beginning to end. The researcher chooses a moment to cut into the action. Time, the speed and depth of change, is an issue at the heart of the study. A complex social organization is a slow-moving machine, seized from time to time by violent eruptions. One cannot foretell anything. A society is neither a fixed structure nor a chaos of free atoms. The butterfly that flaps its wings in Brazil does not cause a tornado in Louisiana, as physicists are supposed to claim. The time of a research project is not the time of the institution that commissions it: the time of the society that reads and evaluates it is different again.

Empirical sociologists know that enormous changes will take place in the course of their research and its publication, extending over five or six years. They do not nurse any illusions that they are going to see everything or produce complete explanations. In the same way, historians know that nothing repeats itself in an identical fashion. They make their choices, setting out a chain of facts that does not have a clear beginning, and never comes completely to an end. They are relativists by the force of circumstances.

When we begin a study, then, we know that it will finish on some more or less distant day, but everything we have studied will go on and will have to adapt. This knowledge must render us modest and prudent. Every field site will have evolved imperceptibly between our entry into the scene that we are examining and our departure – and this process will continue after we have left. We have to be brave enough to admit: "this is how I found my site when I arrived and this is how it was when I left." This is why Becker replaces the excavation of static regularities with an account of relationships in time and space, and of the transformations that result from these. The inevitability of change through time must be captured in understanding the evolution of categories, whose boundaries are necessarily fluid. His studies examine the means by which human groups adapt, accepting or rejecting local norms, developing, or ignoring, the capacities represented by real and living models around them. When we look at someone in action, we can see the way in which their work is shaped by the different groups to which they belong, whether immediately surrounding them or in the background. The situation evolves from one hour to the next. This is a point of critical importance. We live through all of our experiences without necessarily recognizing how they have been shaped by actions in our past, perhaps some years previously, until our memory is jogged by a photo, a letter, a witness that we accidentally run across again. How could I have done that? Did I really think that? Is that person really me? But this is because things have changed in the interim – education and both the frameworks and the substance of scientific and technical knowledge. Art, medicine, scholarly learning are unrecognizable from one generation to another, even from one decade to the next. In medicine, who would have had the idea of self-care just fifty years ago? It is the same in the creative arts. By definition, art belongs to a particular epoch. The conventions that govern it will have been overturned, new publics will have upended the ways of seeing or listening offered by those who hope to be recognized as artists.

A Concentration of Interaction: Processes

The question of time defines the very nature of the empirical sociologist. In acknowledging the importance of time, one places oneself on the side of research. Social science research takes account of the metrics of time: dating systems; rhythms; calendars. No analysis can be taken out of its temporal context. Some specialists would like to see the analysis of situations relieved of the embarrassing contamination of contingency. They simply conceal the relativism of their analyses under a mask of rational experimental criteria. In such circumstances, what value can we attach to the notion of process? We can describe two versions of this concept:

a   The changes and modifications that appear while a case is being studied over a certain period of observation (one or two years is the common duration of presence in a field site). The action in any moment prompts other actions and new contingencies which partly shape the unfolding of the future.

b   The infinite evolution of history as it encounters the weight of institutions with their fixed assumptions and their periodic lurches into new frameworks of operation (cf Faulkner and Becker 2009, pp. 87–113).

If there are several versions of "process," Becker does not choose between them. Whether change is slow or fast, a group or organization is also subject to external shocks and influences (from the diversity of their publics or users, who alter their demands and modify their supplies). Organizations and their champions confront each other, compete or join together for a program of common action. The interaction at the heart of a group, for example, is a succession of alliances, of associations for the successful completion of a project or the resolution of a disagreement. The creation of social or political facts – a legislature, a reform project, a collective product (a political party, an economic program, a film, an exhibition) is both a beginning and an end.

Theoretical Humility

When Becker gives a privileged status to observation, the detailed monograph or the case study, he takes into account the level of abstraction according to social strata (nations, social classes, fractions or families) and the measures of temporality. He finds opportunities to link present actions to their anterior conditions. But this does not happen spontaneously. If one looks for them in his work, one can find classic sources, from newspaper stories to government decisions, from technical descriptions to biographies, typically over a period of about twenty years. The forms of historical consciousness can be fleeting: for many purposes, reference to the last couple of decades is often enough. Such an attitude tempers the itch to reach hasty conclusions or to make excessively categorical recommendations.

Becker clearly rejects theoretical pedantry in favor of modesty. He often says, "I haven't invented anything, I just reassembled the ideas that I found around me." This is a typically pragmatist stance. If one does not grasp the slow rhythms of studying phenomena in painstaking detail, reality will triumph: premature or ill-founded theories will disappear alongside their authors. History – including that of sociology – is unpredictable and its modes of expression are transient. A good place to start is by inverting the tendencies toward scientism. For example, a theory like Durkheim's explanation of suicide is highly contestable because of the inadequacy of its comparisons of international statistics whose validity is more than doubtful. American sociologists like Jack Douglas have dismantled the illusions in statistical accounts of suicide (see Peneff 2009).[2] Even "good" data are vulnerable to social change, to the variability of the methods by which they are measured and the ways of counting. The greatest constructions wash away in the flow of time. If his books have resisted this erosion, it is because Becker has understood that they are capturing moments of history in their stories of interactions. He has not converted this intuition into an intellectual movement. The categories of legitimacy and illegitimacy have been successful as relative values, tied to political or legal systems that are themselves in flux according to the movements and balances between other forces in society.

We should pay more attention to the summaries of Becker's work, which are a good example of how to consider concrete facts in the absence of any claim to assert a "Grand Theory." Reading the table of contents is always a journey into his nonconformity.

> Epistemology has been a similarly negative discipline, mostly devoted to saying what you shouldn't do if you want your activity to merit the title of science, and to keeping unworthy pretenders from successfully appropriating it. The sociology of science, the empirical descendant of epistemology, gives up trying to decide what should and shouldn't count as science... So: this chapter will not be another sermon on how we ought to do science, and what we shouldn't be doing, and what evils will befall us if we do the forbidden things. Rather, it will talk about how ethnographers have produced credible, believable results, especially those results which have continued to command respect and belief... epistemologists have often pretended to such Aristotelian analysis, but more typically deliver sermons.
>
> *(Becker 1996, pp. 54–55)*[3]

Questions and Questionnaires

If we want to use as evidence the responses given by an interviewee, we have to set out the conditions under which the interview took place. We must grasp the impact of the moment and the interactional effects of the exchange. How can these be reconciled with the obligations to truth, and to proof, that we expect from a sociology that gives voice to its actors? Becker, and empirical anglophone sociology, reply that the problem is not exactly one of "giving voice."

Everett Hughes (1971, pp. 507–515) criticized the mistaken and exaggerated claims of bias in interviews. He noted the confusion that arose from mixing up sociological interactions with the sorts of interviews carried out by journalists, or with questioning in ordinary conversation. He emphasizes the considerable differences between these types of engagement. In sociology, we only interview those publics or witnesses who are assumed to be accessible and respectable...to be respectful of "sociology." This stance leaves our informants open to being influenced, if not manipulated, by the sociologist, as someone of a high and certified status, at least as perceived in popular opinion. The number of instances in our professional literature where the sociologist is questioning their social or economic superiors is perhaps no more than 5 percent of all the qualitative interviews conducted in recent years as this method has become more fashionable. This is asymmetry at its worst. Any questioning implies a degree of inequality that is either acknowledged or repressed, a difference that is either experienced or ignored. Of course, a false coziness or a spurious confidence underlined in professional courtesy is often expressed: "I ask questions and you reply to them."

It is inevitable that there will be some influence from the relative social positioning on a scale of value relative to the person asking questions, as a stranger, as a friend or as an adversary. Everyone, at every moment, locates themselves on a scale of social classes according to their consciousness of social stratification. This intuition serves to calibrate our instant evaluations of interaction partners. This intimate assessment has serious consequences, whether we are spending one or more hours face to face (particularly if these hours are being recorded) or are asking for rapid responses, possibly in the street.

The error of objective sociology is to imagine that we could deny, erase or reduce these influences. It is the implication of one of the many illusions about the transparency of the social world that Bourdieu (1999) denounced, as an ethnographer, before giving in to them, particularly in *The Weight of the World*. All professionals, including sociologists, whether in language, in title or in power, think that they are exempt from the constraints of the markers of social status that they manipulate at the expense of other people. Their appearance as members of a social class, a trade, a sex or an age vanishes, as if by magic, when they are carrying out their craft, or can at least easily be nullified. This is a pipedream, as the sociology inspired by Everett Hughes at Chicago has repeatedly shown.

This naïveté is compounded by another. The sociological profession has no way to monitor the validity of the talk that it collects, other than to place blind confidence in the selection that is published. There is no deposit in archives, no effort to make collections of recordings publicly available so that it is possible to assess the tactics and the reciprocal manoeuvers that take place in interviews. This blindness is legitimized by "professional ethics." On this point Becker (2009b) is clear (see also El Miri and Masson 2009).

Sociology is a Science in every respect. End of story, according to those opposed to empirical understanding. And it has such morally unimpeachable advocates. We need not dwell on the problems created for the interview by the feelings of superiority or inferiority linked to the context in which it takes place and the personal histories of the interviewer and the informant. Bourdieu rightly remarked on this when administering questionnaires in Algeria. The whole critique from the Chicago School is based on these claims.

This is not, however, everything. The very process of social interaction itself intervenes. The context and the unfolding talk modify the meaning of the information that is acquired. It is not just the energy, the links between turns, the colorfulness of the oral as against the written text. There is no definitive discursive judgment but a fluid situation which casts its spell. It transforms our craft skills in interaction into a quasi-mystical experience, a faith anchored in the value of "giving voice." All this has been more than well-known and fully established among interactionists for a hundred years – without having any impact on the methodological horizons of French sociology.

This is the legacy to which Becker is heir. If he has not written at length on the subject of interviewing, others have done so before him. He has, though, without joining the argument, added his own contribution – a note in 1953 to assist the cunning interviewer. He describes three techniques in this note, developed from his doctoral thesis, to develop a sort of interview that is half way between skepticism and provocation. He discusses the practice of interviewing and possible tactics, without distinguishing between directive and non-directive approaches. We can use either as the occasion requires. He begins an interview, he says, by asking vague and general questions to identify the topics that the informant seems to know most about, or which are most useful to follow in the course of the interaction. Later, he may interrupt with direct questions, if the conversation seems to be drifting into idle chatter, the sort of superficiality that would mark any relationship with a stranger. At this moment, he plays the innocent, or even the fool, claiming that he does not understand the reply, or believe it, and asking for concrete examples or justifications.

Although other specific skills are available, or could be developed from those of everyday life, Becker, as a matter of principle, rarely interviews people from a social status lower than his own. This may reflect a reluctance to take advantage of mass surveys or a refusal to risk unconscious manipulation: I do not know which reason is the more important.

Becker leans rather toward observing, and listening to discussions, among the dominant classes, mainly in the interest of probing and challenging their implicit resistance to social transparency. He pushes back against their inclination to avoid any sociological investigation of how they, and others, divert questions about their status, or give meaningless answers to these. The techniques used by the upper classes to counter or manipulate investigators are themselves significant. This mistrust of professionally qualified graduate sociologists has shaped the history of research methods, although it has received little attention. Face to face meetings with people from social classes superior to our own are always interesting, even though they are difficult to secure. While the interaction may be tricky to manage, interviews with superiors (judges, physicians, scientists, senior managers, higher police officers, political leaders) are nevertheless valuable, provided one can control the conversation. In any case, they are at least as profitable as those obtained from the ordinary people whose docility we often abuse.

In the short history of sociology, the frame of empirical research has also contained some radical researchers who have claimed that an interview is useless unless it can be fully verified. The details of time and place, the immediate context from which the informant comes, their mental state, all these must be captured if we are to make sense of the content. In the same way, we should specify how our informants perceive the interaction. Do they or do they not accept our agenda? How do they react? All this is essential, if we are to interpret the subjective information that we have collected. This is equally true – although to a lesser degree – for ethnographic conversations, where collaboration includes the possibility of building a relationship of trust over a period of time. There are, then, approaches where the interview is treated as a way of understanding documents or other archival material (press cuttings, reports, political declarations, private correspondence). Another type is the conversation with "the natives." Talk is a natural feature of life in society, in families, in professional groups. Oral relationships are the stuff of mundane existence. We all carry on "interview-conversations" in everyday life, as a matter of curiosity, of personal pleasure or of shared interests. In the course of participant observation, we are constantly talking with other participants in the setting: these exchanges take place *in situ* on various topics, in ways that are more or less improvised, depending upon the context. In the ordinary flow of life, we often ask questions, but these are not forced on anyone. Such informal exchanges do not, then, need the luxury of a detailed textbook or a field manual.

Over the last fifty years, Europe has become bewitched by the idea that interview is a royal road to truth, in sociology and elsewhere. We have trained our students in the idea that the interview represents the main way to acquire knowledge. The only issues are matters of technique, such as recording. The only problems are those of a degree of psychologization that puts us alongside the survey and the opinion poll. Inasmuch as this all seems easy, the contemporary trend appears to be irresistible. The press, other media, the human sciences are saturated with "communication," commentaries on interviews, extracts selected *ad hoc* to prove a prior point. As some acknowledge frankly – and others cynically – this double manipulation (no prior review required of the interviewer before publication and no verification possible by peers or readers) is the trickery of numerous articles and books that have no substance or content other than the discourse. The interview has become information, science and therapy!

We can, however, place the interview directed to a specific ethnographic or historical goal at the other end of the scale, noting the procedures by which it is verified or the collaborative work that is a way of evaluating the interpretation being offered. Like many sociologists, Becker does not place great weight on such a flimsy foundation, but his position is nuanced. He calls for caution in dealing with interviews or statements that are simultaneously public and private.

Where does Becker place himself in relation to the assembly of other kinds of data? He has recently undertaken a broad reflection on the use of numbers and statistical series in society, particularly in the human sciences, in a way that has become obsessional. Along with others (such as Jack Douglas and Aaron Cicourel – in France Alain Desrosières – investigating official statistics) he has denounced the contemporary quantitative madness, the obsession with numbers that has led to the credulous reception of the fictional exactitude of surveys, polls and censuses (the latter in a modern state describe the population at best within a margin of error of around 5–10 percent – if it is sensible to measure an error). Numerous observers (even a paleontologist like Stephen Jay Gould) have commented ironically on this contemporary faith in the power of the modern state. The measurement of an unknowable reality (where cities or areas are inaccessible to its agents) added to the manifest impracticability of a stable accounting is a distraction for the social sciences. This is Becker's current project, which he described at a conference in Geneva.[4]

Is Howard Becker an Interactionist – Or Not?

The relationship among those formerly associated with the University of Chicago Sociology Department is too informal to describe with terms like "School," "Association" or "Union," which imply a consciously shared approach. There are multiple definitions of interactionism and we can find many different examples of its application. At the minimum, it is a matter of focus and of being primarily interested in the relations that link, closely or at a distance, actions, persons and representations. In this sense, we are all interactionists because the substance of all sociology is relationships, comparisons and relativism. This is why sociology studies itself as much as it studies other forms of discourse. Nevertheless, thanks to the geographical separation, and the intellectual distance, between Europe and the United States, what has been defined in France as interactionism has been limited and at times fragmented. This category has become a catch-all. No current methods text does more than assimilate it or oppose it to ethnomethodology or generic qualitative methods. This is a very limited way to understand interactionism.

How should we classify Becker? An interactionist? A symbolic interactionist? A materialist? An ethnographer? A pragmatist? Sociologists do not usually make much of the differences between the study of face to face relationships and the social association of individuals, and the investigation of organizations, institutions or professions. We assume that the direct encounter is essential to interactionism. Groups as informal as thieves and their victims, for example, rarely meet face to face. However, there is an interaction in that space. It is equally rare for police and criminals to meet directly, and yet they think about each other from afar, evaluate their assets and their liabilities, design their maneuvers and finalize their actions in secret. The professions, through their members' actions, judge, assess and compare themselves with each other, modeling their behavior on the basis of interactions that may exist only in imagination. Even the term "symbolic" is contestable other than as a rhetorical device. Interactionism can be defined as symbolic, occasionally as economic or material, sometimes as organizational, or as a form of authority and political violence. Those who carry out all these interactions are far from being symbols. In reality, if "symbolic" signifies an imagined connection, which can be an object of reflection and inserted into a chain of reasoning, then most material and economic interactions are not in the least symbolic, since they are invisible to actors. The balance of power in economic production, in the manufacture of goods, is absent, as are working life, violence, authority. Collaborations, associations and groups of resisters may be partially symbolic if they are regarded as legitimate, reasoning through arguments about issues of representation, discourse or public statements.

Becker does not describe himself as a symbolic interactionist, even if he sometimes uses this as an analytic category. He has developed a way of working that is independent and original, not a paradigm to which he and his admirers should subscribe in order to identify themselves as an academic movement. Although he has been associated with interactionism, a community of scholars that has over half a century developed a body of work, a journal and an annual conference, he has never signed up to any manifesto or any hierarchy of projects. As a result, he has not been much concerned with questions of recruitment or of excommunication. The resistance of European Marxist readers to this kind of free thinking – and censorship by Bourdieu and his acolytes – long blocked Becker from potential audiences in France. Neither Becker nor his associates have much time for textbooks, manuals or dictionaries to define "acceptable" thought. Becker has never written any of these. He rejects grand labels, such as "constructionism," "action theory" or "ethnomethodology," since he sees that each comes in many forms. They display a diversity of practices that make it possible for identities, roles, and inconsistent intellectual positions to co-exist in those situations that seem to demand some kind of mutual engagement or social movement.

To describe Becker as an interactionist is certainly to over-simplify his position. He rejects the label. The grounds for his rejection are clear. He does not discuss actors or agents in isolation. He only deals with primary groups recognizable at different levels of organization and identity. His three great field sites (the school, the medical profession, and the arts and culture) appear through the evocation of vast collectives in which he is personally involved. His earliest research (in his master's and doctoral dissertations under Everett Hughes) describes, as is traditional in sociology, the constraints on action. He does not hesitate to acknowledge the role of authority (the allocation of positions, internal regulations, the power to distribute resources, the status to issue instructions), the role of knowledge (rights, competencies, legality), and the belief in their credibility (trust, legitimacy, relevance). In *Art Worlds* (Becker 1982), indicators and classifications, the definition of the self, are not his first concerns, nor is he interested in critiquing or demolishing them. On the contrary, he questions the invisible sources of authority, the credibility and ingenuity that justify the inertia of the system, particularly in its division of space, its distribution of tasks and its processes of promotion. The phenomena of spontaneous sociability at work are as vital as the organizational culture or the general ambiance, which is in part symbolic. But it is essential to establish whether this factory or this school is like, or unlike, other factories or schools. We can, then, see, in Becker's work as we read it, the chains of production in time and space that have shaped the history of this particular field site. These are not eternal categories: their basis is fragile because the passage of time constantly threatens to destroy the knowledge of sociologists, alter their conclusions and reshape the phenomena that they study. And we can change with him.

Notes

1   The reference is to Dahrendorf (1973). It is intended to contrast with the longer-established model of *homo economicus*, which portrays humans as consistently rational and self-directed actors pursuing individual and subjectively defined goals. *Homo sociologicus* is assumed to seek to fulfil social roles rather than pursuing subjective goals. In this model, the individual can disappear: they are simply the occupant of a role. Becker, and the interactionists generally, resist this and insist on the importance of human agency – roles

are improvised not scripted. It is the contrast between playing jazz and following an orchestral score.

2 Durkheim (1952) had selected suicide as the most individual of all acts in order to demonstrate the effects of society on specific actions through the patterns observable in suicide statistics. In the 1960s and 1970s, interactionist and ethnomethodological investigations argued that these patterns were actually produced by the activities of the social agents responsible for the classification of unexpected deaths. This work was particularly associated with Douglas (1967) in the USA and J. Maxwell Atkinson (1978) in the UK. On the general problems of international death certification, see Vassy et al. (2010).

3 The original citation is to a slightly different version of the chapter which appeared as "Epistémologie de la recherche qualitative" in Pessin, A. and Blanc, A., eds (2004, p. 62). This particular passage does not seem to have been altered from its first appearance.

4 This paragraph describes the substance of the work that Becker (2017) published in *Evidence*. The references are to Douglas (1967), Cicourel (1964), and Desrosières (1993).

5

PROFESSOR BECKER'S APPROACH TO TEACHING

The list of Becker's principal concepts is not exhausted by his "classic" notions, such as moral entrepreneur, labeling and deviance, working together, career, informal apprenticeship, credibility, the power of inertia, worlds and representations, talking about society. To complete the story, let us now examine their diffusion through teaching. Becker has published five books of advice on "methodology," without counting various prefaces or presentations. In these, he sets out, with passion, an original position on how to improve teaching and the craft skills of researchers. Ever since his doctoral thesis he has emphasized the importance of teaching, in papers like "The Career of the Chicago Public School Teacher," "The Teacher in the Authority System of the Public School," "Social Class Variations in the Teacher-Pupil Relationship."[1] His ideas are further developed in these books:

Sociological Work (Becker 1970)
Doing Things Together (Becker 1986)
Writing for Social Scientists: How to Start and Finish Your Thesis, Book, or Article (Becker 2007b)
Tricks of the Trade: How to Think About Your Research While You're Doing It (Becker 1998)

Being curious about Becker's approach to undergraduate teaching, with young people in their early twenties during their final year of study, I asked him if I could sit in on the classes for one of his semester-long courses while I was visiting Chicago.[2] This was a transformative experience for me, which I have described in a book of tributes to Howard Becker (Pessin and Blanc 2004).

The course was quite the opposite of a magisterial lecture, being more like a discussion among peers. The students interrupted and exchanged ideas. At each class, Becker had a main theme: a book, an event, something in the news, an incident in the university, a dissertation or a piece of work by a student. He focused the discussion on some unexpected aspect of the social world that would be known to the audience. His objective was to transform observation of everyday life into sociological problems. But it was not just a question of his subject matter. The style and tone of his pedagogy were just as important:

> He always arrived punctually at nine o'clock,[3] strolling in, chatting with whichever student he had met by chance at the exit from the subway and who had come, like him, from downtown Chicago. A casual jacket, a check shirt, jeans with a gunslinger's belt, a book in his hand: none of this is very orthodox and certainly not the style of other professors who joined the faculty at the same time, with their suits and ties and attaché cases. But this relaxed look was not that of an intellectual of the left, whether angry or thoughtful, nor that of a master with an entourage. His classroom was surprising. He refused to teach in a traditional lecture theatre with a pulpit, pews and desks ...he had chosen an obscure room in the basement of a university building, a room that no-one else wanted. This dark room, with only an air vent in place of a window, without formal seating, without a table for books, whose door opened onto a corridor that served as a store for the maintenance crew, this was his preferred teaching space. It was strangely furnished with battered seating apparently purchased from a junk shop...Everyone took their place in a circle. Some students preferred to sit on the floor with their backs to the wall... from time to time a student would get up and go to the vending machine for a coffee. Everything was in a low key but the whole atmosphere was one of rapt attention.
>
> *(Peneff 2004, p. 16)*

Because I have gone into detail elsewhere, I will not extend this discussion, except to make a few additional comments. I will underline, on the basis of the conversations that I had with his students, the importance of their written reports – one every two weeks – and Becker's comments on these short texts. The volume of observations routinely expected from students, and the commentary on them, seemed fundamental to Becker's approach. It appeared to me – and the students confirmed this – that the development of a critical intellect in these young people emerged from the trust that he showed in their knowledge of the social world and the lack of distance between him and the members of the class. This was achieved through open discussions and from his expectation that there would be collective engagement with every student's presentations or observations from the field. Each in their turn, the students were expected to take the role of critic, note-taker and counsellor to their colleagues through written advice or constructive collaboration (recommending reading, suggesting interpretations of data). This was what made the course a master-class in the method of observation, an authentic and lived experience of solidarity...and sometimes of passion.

If you can only read one of his pedagogic works, I would recommend *Writing for Social Scientists* (Becker 2007b), which is an informal summary of the positions that I have already set out. It is not necessary to explain these varied texts in great detail. There are no curt directions, no rigid instructions. Instead, we find practical tips and examples drawn from the situation of (young) researchers. How can we write? How can we revise? How can we get published? The sections on "Ideas" and "Examples" in *Telling about Society* (Becker 2007a) are equally addressed to a wider readership. He never forgets to be concerned about the survival of the discipline. How should we pass sociology on from one generation to the next? This is expressed particularly in his concern for "how not to teach the subject."

Why is Becker so passionate about the education of young sociologists? And why is he so critical of the places where scholarship is practiced, when you could say that he was a perfect "output" and not a frustrated victim. Consider his titles: "A School is a Lousy Place to Learn Anything in" (Becker 1972) or "What's Happening to Sociology?" (Becker 1979). These are stinging contributions. In the 1960s, he foresaw the failure of a formalistic and rigid approach to pedagogy and questioned the extent to which we could promote learning exclusively within institutions. Pedagogy is too important to be left to pedagogues, he remarked ironically.

Observation without Dogma

The general features of participant observation are now sufficiently well known in France that we do not need to revisit them here. We have made Becker into the high priest of observation but we must take a more nuanced approach. The practices of observation, he notes, are not immutable: they vary with national cultures, the nature of the publics involved and the historical conditions under which the investigations take place. He accepts the need for adaptability, eclecticism, a diversity of involvements, of selective reading and of discussions with professionals. Each monograph is a step forward and not free play. We can never have too many methods, and the freedom to use them. He is opposed to doctrinaire statements and has never produced a manual or textbook. His courses and advice swarm with suggestions, examples rather than commands, and flexible explanations. He is not afraid to talk about his setbacks. He only discusses certain aspects of any particular observation.

As a method, observation requires a strong element of improvisation, so his advice is consistently that of simply going to see what is happening. This means putting oneself into a setting, spending time there and acquiring experience of it. He appreciates the "method" of Nicolas Hatzfeld (2002) who carried out two periods of participant observation on the same assembly line at Peugeot ten years apart. When he returned, he was, as an "independent" university researcher, able to get unfettered access to the archives of the trade unions and the management. Becker approved the idea of beginning observations as a paramedic coming into a hospital and ending up in the cellars, examining the organization's archives. There are no rules. The imagination required for participant observation never dries up. Other contributions emerge into the light of day from the pivotal experience of participation, however limited this may be. This approach to observation is currently not well understood. Perhaps it will become better known thanks to the work of review and synthesis by Daniel Céfaï (2003).

No Limits to Participation

A more interesting question might be: up to what point can we engage in observation? How can we participate without going to the extreme in studies of delinquency or criminality? Can we share in the preparation, take part in the event or just be a bystander to the action? If the last is impossible, as it often is in closed social worlds, what should we do? It is difficult to define what constitutes participation, a fluid term. Becker would say that this places too much importance on engagement or the degree of proximity. Full participation can be inconvenient. Inside knowledge can be useful, but this is not always the case and is not systematically required. "Taking the role of the other" is an ambiguous formula. A single individual does not represent the world view of a small group whose collective vision evolves in the course of action, is reassembled in rationalizations produced after the event, and in the memories set down in written statements or witness reports. Yet another confusion emerges: who is telling this story, who is the author of this "point of view"? The subject, a witness or a neutral third party? This is not clear, even in the more restrictive approach taken by the ethnomethodologists. How can we grasp another's point of view, their most intimate thoughts, their reasoning and their justifications for action without running the risk of psychologizing or focusing on transient and ephemeral verbalizations?

In adopting a flexible position, Becker is convinced that it is a piece of good fortune to get to know a field before entering it. This may seem like a statement of the obvious – but how important it is! To become, for example, an artist or a practical user of an instrument (a piano, a camera, a theatre) and to master some of the associated technical or organizational problems gives him a head start so that his critiques never deal unfairly with the fields that he covers. In the course of each period of observation, he freely adopts several levels of participation depending on his degree of visibility and the local circumstances (ease of access, length of stay). His observations span primary data, like the interactions between people and organizations, and secondary data – conventions and rules, applied politics, rights and duties: often these are only disentangled from the field notes long after the event. What interests him is not on the gigantic scale of ideal types: it is the practical accomplishment of organization from case to case of actions and the exercise of powers. He learned, from an early point, that successful outcomes, and, consequently, the ability to initiate projects, are generally achieved by those who have the most authority to impose their model of scientific production by controlling the means of demonstrating the greatest degree of legitimacy. In contrast, the observer is best placed to uncover hidden monopolies or personal gains from work that is diverse and collective. Like many others, he declares that the competition for career advantages between sociologists leads them to work in isolation and to exaggerate their rivalry. In this context, his recommendations, even the ones that he does not intend to be taken seriously, are salutary and bracing. His open approach is not challenged by those who prefer more sophisticated conceptions. Today, as ever, polemics have no other goal than to claim a title for a new player in the arena. Despite his discreet reservations, we never find Becker trying to exclude people or criticize others in a personal way. Everyone has their place in Becker's democratic universe, which is in all cases opposed to hierarchy and respectful of the freedoms of every researcher.

Objectivity or Neutrality?

A more serious challenge is the one that is sometimes put to us: whose side are we on? Are we conservatives or progressives? On the right or on the left? Becker replies to these questions that we are on the side of independence from such artificial categories. As for an ethical stance, rather than claiming an unattainable objectivity, Becker prefers to talk about a gradual improvement in our neutrality. The only good answer that we can give to such questions, in his view, is to struggle against the tendency to make snap judgments and take sides. Putting our immediate self-interest at a distance, as a result of our epistemological choices, is closely linked to a view of our publics, our readers, and those who make use of our conclusions. They must decide for themselves whether or not to accept our ideas. In consequence, our definitions of good sociology are determined by our various interests in the success of our publications, our invited lectures, and our professional honors. Neutrality entails acknowledging these inevitable tendencies. Becker (2007a, pp. 109–147) comments on these, in his usual indirect fashion in two chapters that have generally received little attention from those who have written about him. The political implications of his conceptions of deviance have been criticized by sociologists from both left and right. The former charge him with supporting the established order since he does not have an explicit project of struggling against injustices, inequalities and other disadvantages by being an advocate for subversive representations. Becker (1966) joined this debate in his paper, "Whose Side Are We On?" Are we on any side or everyone's? In truth, we are on the side of sociology, is his reply. We are neither beneath nor above the flux of everyday life. If we are skilled in our craft, we try to grasp the totality of a situation: our role is to illuminate, to analyze to the fullest the actions and perceptions of society that we find there. Our personal feelings remain outside that part of our trade. We aim to describe in order to understand. Without judgments!

It is more reasonable to assert that we are on the side that gives us most data or information that is new or useful. We can write a book full of information – as the historians know how to do – without giving an opinion on the implications of a political or moral action. The only commitment, according to Becker, is to the depth of our case study, to the extension of knowledge, and to the increase in source material. The argument that he challenges is that of established authority. Who is issuing condemnations or disqualifications in asserting "This is not sociology." Who is doing the judging? Employers or education authorities, famous authors, academic associations, readers, the mass media? Right now, all of them have a small part in this process.

Conceptions of Research

We have shown that Becker has developed an approach that is rich in new ideas, particularly about improving writing, teaching and the choice of research topics. These innovations can be summed up in three propositions:

(1) First, a style stripped of professional complexity. Throughout his career, the strength of Becker's work has been in avoiding the epistemological quarrels of the genre... "this is not science, that is not a good method" but rather to devote himself, as we have seen, to projects that are direct and bounded. This is what has allowed him to anticipate issues, to see the future before others do, in the places where he directs his attention. It is not enough to seek out the *avant-garde*: we must take it forward through a succession of analyses. He has achieved this in three programs. First, as we have noted, in the investigation of types of consumption that were initially forbidden and then tacitly tolerated. Second, he turned to professional education, to questions of work and identity, themes that were less fashionable in 1960 than they are today. Finally, he became interested in the explosion in the forms and contents of markets for art, which he saw as a success for mass culture. In 1950, he had already seen that the coming century would be that of music (from classical to jazz or rock, without overlooking the French genre of *chanson*) and of the image (photography, television, cinema). The commonplace nature of his specific choices seemed hard to argue with, but they were perplexing for Europeans. The chapters (in Becker 2007a) which discuss the questions of "truth," of plausibility, of the honesty of sociology, clash with the formal rationalists. This may be justified, as he argues, by the way in which history, geography or demography have achieved credibility thanks to their abandonment of any normative claims. They have taken the most direct route by favoring description which, for him, is never exhausted. Let yourself be saturated by new facts. Take the paths into unexplored territories. These are some of his recommendations – without reference to commercial interests. His books do not declare what is right or wrong. He does not make prophesies about the future. He concludes that all sociology is utopian because events cannot be foreseen. And yet, says Becker, studying events does achieve something in refining the spirit of analysis. Others say this just extends the use of questionnaires to explore social reality. Of course, Becker implies the abandonment of causal relations in a simple mechanistic form. Neutrality is not a contingent truth but the expression of a form of creativity without prior beliefs, without crusades, aiming at a better knowledge of interactions that are numbered in millions. From the outset this new approach distinguished itself from the functionalism otherwise favored by US sociologists.

(2) Finding a research topic. Becker's autonomy in defining possible research themes has brought him to seize upon the underground evolution of great cities, of the people who live in them, of their nocturnal life, and of the work of the young people who have been recruited to all sorts of new services. This is a distinctive window on the world of urban sociology. We can call this inclination authorial curiosity or a refusal to tread well-worn paths.

The result is to deinstitutionalize the social sciences, something which he began in a tentative fashion and then adopted as an explicit goal. No one thought of making a living out of sociology at the beginning of the twentieth century, at least not in Europe. Such a project, such an ambition could only become a dogma through instruction. It was not possible to conceive of spreading a rebellious or critical spirit through the established system of educational institutions. Sociology was a young science, independent-minded and uncomfortable with orthodoxy, threatened by the risk of being colonized by scholasticism. Unfortunately, the outcome was a drift into bureaucracy where research was transformed into a task for statisticians or information scientists. It is this sort of work that is still, regrettably, produced today by researchers tied into partial and quantifiable projects, whose duration is that of a specific grant or an administrative contract. The task of teaching has become more of a burden, and the load has been mechanically distributed to young instructors, who have not had time to acquire much experience in the field. Becker has succeeded in escaping the authority of heavyweight university structures. This is how has been able to wander around topics of his own choosing, problems that accord with his own tastes. He advertises this freedom loudly and at length. Around 1970, he opened a window into the universe of resources that he draws on: cinema, photography or internet graphics, comic strips. To an already extensive inventory of research, he added the new skill of visual sociology derived from photojournalism (Becker 2007a, pp. 186–203). After music, he became an apostle of the image (as he put it during a conference at the Free University of Brussels in 2010). He became the organizer and curator of several photographic exhibitions (*Exploring Society Photographically*) around fifteen leading anthropologists who had used this method including Gregory Bateson, Margaret Mead and Douglas Harper.[4]

The facts have proved him right. Today, iconography is inescapable. Neither geography nor ethnology can dispense with it. The photograph is no longer an illustration that is accessory to a story, a distraction for the mind, but a document with the same status as an archive or a field note. How is it that sociology should have been the last discipline to resist accepting such material reproductions of the social into its canon of work when they are so central? After his studies of photography, Becker has worked for the introduction of a little more fantasy from a less austere discipline. The idea of acting out, together with a colleague, in a theatrical sense, a scientific communication, as he did at one conference, instead of carefully reading a paper, was not a mere whim on his part.

(3) Systematic comparison was his third original contribution. Becker pushes this to its limits. By placing into the same analytic framework, a sociological text, a

documentary photo, a realist novel, demographic or economic statistics, he has added to the palette with which he depicts his subjects. In the same way, he has more recently appealed for painting, cartoons and comic strips to be added to the sociologist's toolkit. He studies these media to tell their own story. Their creation brutally exposes failures, abandoned discoveries, successes that were still-born. His thinking involves investigating the preferred instruments of each resource and establishing the parallels between their internal logic and their expressive character. He describes a set of apparently unconnected phenomena, such as statistical accounts represented in diagrams or algebraic symbols. These constitute a form of scientific ethnography that tells its own story. The imagined strength of statistical "proof" rests in the way that tables or coefficients are presented more than in the means by which they are calculated. What distinguishes his approach from the traditional internal critiques to be found in our textbooks emerges from his analytic approach to labels and classifications. As he usually does, once a problem has been launched against the flow, he immediately moves on. He does not hand out keys to an answer but waits for the public reaction before returning to the high ground of his reasoning. As for the rest, we must try to infer this from his writing, while taking note of his sly amusement at our efforts!

Music in "Society"

Let us extend our bold interpretation of Becker's comparative mood by looking at two of his soulmates who were both thinkers and musicians – Jean-Jacques Rousseau and Max Weber. In contemporary societies music is a growing phenomenon, a link between generations. Becker uses it in teaching as resource for metaphors accessible to the young. He suggests that we should "write as we sing" or "revise as we listen," encouraging pleasant sounds. There are curious parallels with these earlier social thinkers and musicians: they shared his inclination toward a simple style of writing and clarity of expression, an inclination that is not general among sociologists. It is unarguable that his tendency, to join a simple and elegant style to apparently lightweight content, is deceptively anodyne because its meaning has been worked at with the greatest of care. The lightness of a sentence does not signify either a lack of description or a weakness of argument. The choice of form and the name given to the case are critical. Knowing how to label a piece, having a rich repertoire of possibilities, are important for defining the key terms of our trade. The wording of headings and subheadings is intentionally designed to evoke a sense of the familiar while maintaining the forms of learning. An approach that is brief, imaginative and expressive has become Becker's signature. An analysis of the content of his titles shows that "How to come up with a title in the social sciences" would well match his already famous *Writing for Social Scientists*.

If we may dare make the comparison, let us note that Jean-Jacques Rousseau, a fine musician, set out, from his perspective, a theory of musical writing expressing social and civic purposes. It was the way he mainly made his living, as a copyist or composer of operas. He devised a new notation (stave, scale, interval) that would, he thought, be more rational for composition and make it easier to distribute music. However, he ran up against the institutions and the previously undisputed master-figure of Jean-Philippe Rameau. Rousseau's entries on music in Diderot's encyclopedia, although edited in response to the demands of d'Alembert, still remain celebrated. Who knows whether this setback in the musical field, at the beginning of his career, might not have been the origin of his shining *Discourse on the Arts and Sciences*, written at the same time as an entry to a competition run by the Academy of Dijon?[5] This well-known episode combines the impact of the hierarchy of credibility with the inertia of institutions, both key themes in Becker's work. In any case, Rousseau's full and lengthy sentences are rich in sounds, and thus in rhetorical force.

To extend the analogy between music and writing, we might look to Max Weber (1958) and his book on the sociology of music. Weber's general thesis is familiar. Without an inherent sense of classification or a scale of relative values, the music of the West developed a harmonic form that had no natural superiority to the melodic forms of music created elsewhere and reflecting other ways of organizing sound-space. In music, the response to the physical vibrations that make up sounds is not universal but is the product of a particular civilization and the historical "forms" that it has constructed. The types of rationalization in art are no different from those in economic or political life and their valuation is equally relative. Western sociology is no more rational than Oriental sociology: Arabs, Chinese, and Indians are not exempt from the logics of social analysis. The correlation is obvious. Becker understood this intuitively as a very young man, through his experiences with jazz and classical music. In his personal history, the musician sometimes influences the sociologist – and sometimes the reverse. In any case, his references and his examples overlap, as in his most recent major comparative work (Becker 2007a). In this, we can see when and where the elaboration of these rationalizations has diverged. Becker finds these homologies at the heart of many social "discourses," whether visual or narrative: stories, images, calculations, designs, photographs, novels, mathematical treatises, statistical accounts, maps. Where Weber saw rationalization and sophistication in such places, Becker sees the complex representation of images as more than technique. He is not an idealist in disguise. He is deeply concerned about the elements that are stabilized by convention and by the necessity of specific empirical support for this.

The Style of Writing

Becker (1974) notes the simultaneous birth of our discipline and of photography, almost two hundred years ago in an amusing incident, which is briefly described in the Preface to the *Encyclopaedia Universalis*.[6] When various critics and philosophers, around 1840, revived the old idea of studying "society" in its own right, creating a discipline whose expertise would lie in understanding the whole, they set off a craze in France and in America, the sites of the main democratic revolutions, whose affinity was noted by de Tocqueville. There was clear recognition of the need to replace the excessively speculative approach of social philosophy by more secular arguments. In each of these societies, urbanization, industrialization, and social conflicts stimulated demands for an independent body of knowledge about their organization and internal relationships.

This is how sociology emerged in the middle of the nineteenth century. It offered a rational basis for a politicized historical narrative, written by intellectuals who were socially engaged but excluded, or marginalized, from state power. Following moral philosophy and law, social science became a new religion, albeit one with a secular character.[7] In establishing itself, the young discipline was obliged to align with existing technologies, such as mathematics, which it mimicked in order to make its numerical measures seem more secure. The young "science" took a different path in Chicago, as it escaped from the shadow of political philosophy and became associated with the social transformations of the twentieth century. Becker was one of the engineers of this turn.

In another challenge to the norms imposed by one generation on its successors, Becker has not followed the conventional modes of publication, whether in terms of academic books (on single topics, focused, closing down problems with apparently logical internal boundaries) or journal articles, with their prescribed lengths and scholarly footnotes. He has adapted these formats. His preferred mode of publication is a short article, a digest of details (ten or so pages), a brief note. He has commented that there is a gap in publishing between the article and the book. This reflection came to him from watching Erving Goffman write, creating texts that did not conform to the canonical format but averaged about sixty pages. In the same fashion, *Outsiders* (Becker 2008) brings together four articles, each dealing with two or three different agendas of problems. Always attracted by freedom and innovation when he was a student, he escaped the conventional shackles that constrain publication. Several of his other books are made up from articles that are united by bridging themes, the accidents of presentation, and a sideways look at previous work. Publication formats, he says, should adapt to the new outputs from research, not the reverse. While this attitude might have led to the rejection of his manuscripts by some editors, this would, for him, be annoying but not devastating. You will always find a publisher somewhere, he advises young scholars struggling to get published. Commissioning editors will give way once you have acquired a reputation, even if this takes a little time to achieve. We might also add that it is better to be part of a group when attempting to reform the traditional models of publication (length, unity of subject matter) and of a writing style derived from philosophy. There was a group at Chicago who did not want to write like their contemporaries at Harvard or Columbia, the great rival universities. Becker discusses this in relation to the bold terminological innovations made by Erving Goffman (Becker 2007a, pp. 223–237). These transformations of style made it possible for *Asylums* (Goffman 1968, first US publication in 1961) and *Outsiders* (first published in 1963) to become cult texts among undergraduates. All of this produced a lively moment of disruption.

Becker would be the first to say: here are our recipes and our techniques, and this is what they imply about what is understood or implicit in our demonstrations. We must, however, be equally bold in expressing our doubts about the models of quantification that we have inherited – foundations on which we have built while remaining ignorant about them. As I have said, Becker is currently working on our obsession with numbers and on the invasion of our thinking by statistics that are not "fake" but simply mediocre.[8] The result is not a renunciation of calculation or counting – on the contrary, as I have previously acknowledged (Peneff 2009). Becker does not offer an answer to questions about the nature of our discipline: Is it the queen of the sciences?[9] Should it prove its worth through prediction, by agreement on its core concepts, or by the reproducibility of its findings? All objectives that are either presumptuous or unachievable.

The essential question is a different one: if sociology is something other than a special part of the human sciences, then it must find a new role. In this unknown territory, Becker moves stealthily. Without shouting from the rooftops, he overturns the hierarchy of the social sciences in *Telling about Society* (Becker 2007a). On what basis? Does he make a ringing declaration derived from German philosophy? Not at all! The book opens with some funny stories about tourists lost in San Francisco puzzling over their maps and the cartographer's symbols. Is he just being provocative or is there something to learn from this anecdote? Of course it is the latter, much in the style of William James, the pragmatist philosopher, who often began an important book with an invented story. James's radical pragmatism and empiricism are not treated as sacred texts in France. However, they make themselves felt in other ways. Can the French definition of sociology be sustained? Can our discipline survive for another century? Nothing is less certain! Humanity did not wait for the appearance of sociology to be interested in social organization and collective life. It explored these topics by different means on other continents. Political doctrines, art, religion, kinship systems, are all attempts to make sense of society. The core idea is that there are multiple ways of communicating within any society about its condition, such that it is difficult to invent them anew in each generation. To paraphrase Jack Goody's (2006) discussion of the historical narratives that we have stolen from those who do not live in the West, the *theft of sociologies* is today obscured by a mask of European ethnocentrism that distorts the forms of reflexivity developed elsewhere. Becker, then, encourages us to follow a medley of genres (art, photography, fiction, algebra) in order to understand how other civilizations have a sociology that is as scientific as our own. It is up to us to solve the puzzle from the clues that Becker scatters behind himself. In his aversion to syntheses and systems, Becker sometimes only gives us hints, a few allusions, some starting points, through which we can escape from the fog of our own thoughts.

Becker remains insistent that questions of style and form are not marginal. These are, in his view, essential if we seriously intend to communicate our thinking. He has devoted several books and articles to this argument. To write simply, to be inspired by crystal-clear story-tellers – he cites Perec and Calvino whose work he knows well – this is not to renounce sociology.[10] The processes by which sociologists justify their work in literary terms, or by the use of mathematical reasoning, do not mean that they have to write in a complicated way in order to appear "scientific." By comparison with his contemporaries, Becker writes in a style that is much less sophisticated and formal. Any approach to writing always has some element of arbitrariness but he has vigorously resisted the charges of writing in a way that is too simple, or even simplistic, that have been made against him:

> This way of writing is also tied to my conception of sociology. If I can refer to Hughes again, I will say that sociology does not find out things that no-one would already have known. You could say that it is not so much a question of revealing what has been hidden, but of finding something extra, in the sense of going into places where other people have not perhaps gone…This is not, then, an extraordinary and magical activity and there is not the slightest need for an esoteric vocabulary.
> *(Interview with Briand and Chapoulie in Briand and Peretz 1996, p. 77)*

By defending the right of readers to understand a work, by writing it in a way that is not solemn, not pretentious, and not posing as a revelation from a master, Becker extends the possibilities of engaging non-specialists. In doing this, he has, in a modest fashion, popularized many elements of our discipline. Without setting out to do so, he has created an "interpretive community," a public that regularly reads and adopts his work. He has reached beyond sociology to four large readerships that he has drawn into his analytic enterprise. We can see this from the public attention that he draws for his lectures in France. He has united several constituencies attracted by the vision set out in his writing:

a   Knowledge workers who are applying and ultimately reflecting his norms in the widest sense: jurists, police, judges, educators, legal journalists, social workers, sociologists.
b   Artists, musicians, instrumentalists, journalists and art critics, cultural commentators, collectors, museum and gallery professionals, dealers, publishers and promoters of cultural events.
c   Educators, school leaders, teachers – in elementary and high schools, instructors, civil servants, university students, and even pupils in high school.
d   Literary journalists, photographers, designers, news reporters, those whose hobby is working with documents or biographies.

To each of these interpretive communities, Becker says: "You know some things better than I do, but, together with others, I know how to make comparisons. We have time to elaborate these together and to place my experience beside yours." This is the basis of his success with a diverse public. Authors are often puzzled by the tastes and enthusiasms of their readership. These are often no clearer to publishers or commentators. These last have today isolated sociology, marketed only to captive publics, especially students, in the form of textbooks, readers and dictionaries. In presenting its choices as unquestionable, the publishing industry restricts authors in the social sciences to those topics that are "media friendly" social problems or which are spuriously "engaged" social criticism. Sociology should be a pursuit for intelligent people, a joy, one of the alternatives offered to the cultured citizen.

But, for apprentices or students, it is difficult to resolve the dilemma between writing simply and producing the kind of jargon or wordiness required to pass examinations. Becker discusses this problem in an interview with Alain Müller (2009). In commenting on the question of what kind of writing should be adopted for which public, he suggests that it is the responsibility of dissertation committees to engage with the student's style of writing.[11]

HB: A specific community including only the adviser, the candidate and the jury, that is to say three, four or five people. I mean, that's a tiny community. I don't care at that moment if anyone in the world reads, likes or doesn't like my work, only these five people. Because they are the ones who say "Yes" or "No."

AM: So you would suggest the students play the game of writing a bit about theories?

HB: Well, if they must, they must.

AM: The "users" want this to appear in the work that they read.

HB: The only thing is, students very often exaggerate what the professors want.

AM: And forget that they are the best specialists in their own fieldwork.

HB: Right. Because I want to warn them that what they are doing now is not what they will be doing for the rest of their professional lives and that they should be careful not to learn very bad habits. Because that's exactly what happens. We train people – I never did but my colleagues did – to write in this horrible style that will never be any use to them. But the students think, "Well, yes, this is the right way, this is the way you are supposed to, if you want people to think you are smart." And you get a terrible vicious circle because they write as they have been taught for the journals they publish in. If I glance at the journals to see how it should be done, I only see this style of writing. The journals don't have any choice, because everything that comes in has been written in the same style and they publish it. If you really want someone who is not familiar with this arcane and esoteric style to be able to read those articles, you need to think seriously about the problem. I mean, it's very different if you write a book as opposed to an article for a journal. At the end of the day, authors have to find buyers: if no-one wants to read their books, no-one will buy them. This is a strong pressure from publishers to write books in a way that anyone can read them. As far as journals are concerned, the libraries will buy them anyway and no-one really cares whether the stuff that is published is readable or not. This is where we are today. As you see, Alain, you have pressed a hot button there!

Notes

1 All these papers are collected in Becker (1970).
2 In a personal communication, Becker notes that the class that Peneff actually joined was for first year graduate students, who were more or less committed to becoming sociologists.
3 Becker says it was ten o'clock…
4 Becker says he only organized one: "It's too hard to do!" The exhibition was held at the Leigh Block Gallery, Northwestern University, Evanston, IL from October 16–November 29, 1981. See Becker (1981).
5 Jean-Jacques Rousseau (1712–1778) is best known as a philosopher and social theorist. However, he was also a significant musician, composer and critic. He devised a system of notation based on numbers and symbols, rather than lines on a stave. This was presented to the French Academy of Sciences in 1742. He argued that this would be easier for printers to set and beginners to learn. This would help to make music more widely accessible (Simon 2004). The system was dismissed by the Academy, although Rousseau was praised for his ingenuity. It was also strongly criticized by J.-P. Rameau (1683–1764), the most influential French composer of the day. This began a hostility between the two men that continued for many years, particularly in the "*Querelle des Bouffons*" between 1752 and 1754, over the rival merits of Italian and French approaches to operatic composition. Rousseau also used the entries on music that he wrote for Diderot's *Encyclopédie* to attack Rameau – the reference here is to the intervention of D'Alembert (1717–1783), the co-editor, in toning them down. *The Discourse on the Arts and Sciences* was written in response to an essay competition run by the Academy of Dijon in 1749. The topic was: "Has the restoration of the sciences and arts contributed to the purification of morals?" Rousseau's answer was negative. It was an early articulation of his argument that humans were by nature happy and good but were corrupted by society and its institutions, including the arts and sciences. Peneff is suggesting that this analysis reflected Rousseau's own encounter, as an outsider, with the Academy and with the French elite, represented by Rameau. The Academy is identified with the inertia of institutions and Rameau with the hierarchy of credibility.
6 The *Encyclopaedia Universalis* is a scholarly French-language encyclopedia of similar status to the *Encyclopædia Britannica*. See http://www.encyclopaedia-universalis.fr/ [accessed January 29, 2018]. Auguste Comte (1798–1857) was the first to use the term "sociology," in a published work, as the label for a field of study, in 1838. Louis Daguerre (1781–1851) published his method for fixing an image on a metal plate in 1839.
7 Comte founded a "Church of Humanity" intended to displace organized religion with secular rituals intended to promote mutual understanding and social solidarity. In the late nineteenth and early twentieth century, this had an international network of "temples" but seems to have become extinct during World War II.
8 See Becker (2017).
9 The reference is to Comte's claim that sociology was the supreme science because of the way in which all other forms of knowledge were ultimately grounded in society.
10 Georges Perec (1936–1982) was a French novelist, filmmaker and essayist. See Becker (2007a, pp. 252–269). Italo Calvino (1923–1985) was an Italian journalist and writer. See Becker (2007a, pp. 270–284).
11 In many European countries and the USA, PhD students have a main adviser and a committee of senior faculty who oversee the progress of their dissertation or thesis. After an oral defense, which is held in public in Europe, the committee determine whether the work is good enough to award the degree. One or two external assessors may join the committee at the very end of the process and add their voices to the collective judgment. In the UK, PhD students more typically have a pair of advisers who work with them to develop their thesis, which is then read and assessed in a private oral defense by a senior faculty member from the same university and a person of similar status from another university. It is the judgment of these two individuals that determines whether or not the degree is awarded.

6

BECKER IN FRANCE

A Good Use of Franco-American Comparisons

Becker foresaw at an early point the dangers of sociology evolving into a pale replica of a science. It would be necessary to restrain this impulse before it got out of hand. How much time would be wasted in excommunications! How many pages would be covered in print to position oneself against some doctrine or some rival! A favorite occupation for those who have given up the calling of research is to regulate the work of others. Becker continues to research to show that it is our only reason to exist. Petty political arguments, and investigations subsidized by public funds, have led sociology to be subservient to the partisan expectations of the political class, and the mundane accounting requirements of public administration. "How did we get into this mess?" French sociologists ask themselves. We might reply: "by becoming the authors of our own careers, and dependent on the state, which now calls us to account for ourselves." The idea of writing a book on a social issue is becoming more and more obsolete. Young people are turning elsewhere to understand society. Sociology is indeed mortal. It may now have run its course. As Alain Pessin (2017, p. 85) has rightly said: "When it [sociology] ceases to exist, that will not be because it has exhausted all the problems it is concerned with, or because they have exhausted themselves; it will be simply because people will feel a need, for reasons that are still entirely unforeseeable, to agree on another way of telling each other our stories, stories that are interested in the way we do things together."

While most practicing sociologists give up fieldwork at around the age of forty-five, in order to lead a team or to go into administration, Becker has continued to do research. Of course, he has benefited from free time, but he has achieved this by not getting involved in the governance of the discipline or taking part in a pointless competition for power. The rejection of an institutional yoke does not imply rejecting a proper professional position. It is more complicated when one is both within and outside university bureaucracy. Today, as these constraints have become crushing, and the burden of institutional tasks has much increased, he calls for a rejection of the intrusion of the "market" or toadying to funders. How can things change? Becker suggests a middle way. Do not let yourself be intimidated by a false hierarchy; do not think that the accumulation of administrative powers or reputation within the discipline is essential for a career. Remaining a researcher is an act of choice. Not leaving fieldwork to salaried collaborators shows the humility of someone who has always tested himself against a new problem whenever he has stepped up to the plate. Finally, while Becker is an indefatigable producer of original ideas and materials, he has constructed a public, an audience for his work, without seeking publicity. For what purpose and to what end?

Part of the answer is his affirmation: "Good sociology is that which, at a given moment, is useful, interesting and practical." These three criteria speak to our times. They are particularly attractive to young people who feel marginalized or excluded. He has rehabilitated a way of doing sociology that is critical without being simplistic, sophisticated without being elitist. The place of our knowledge within the academy is an accident of the history of ideas, not an irreversible fact. The emphasis on university-based learning does not make us stronger. On the contrary, engagement with the tasks of management associated with professional honors is a barrier to engagement in research and of little value to students.

This is why Becker refused to be a candidate for the presidency of the American Sociological Association, the most prestigious office that it offers, one occupied by both Goffman and Burawoy as the price of their acceptance by the "establishment."[1] For Becker, the loss of independence, the time wasted on the bureaucracy of the profession, the duties of representation, all seemed unbearable. Nevertheless, he has accepted temporary honorary positions in a learned society, the *Society for the Study of Symbolic Interaction*, which is more like a bunch of mates; together with others, he also founded and co-directed *Visual Sociology*. His refusal to direct a research group, to edit a journal,[2] his avoidance of media appearances[3] do not signal his isolation – far from it! He happily accepts invitations to speak when he is invited. He takes part in conferences and seminars. He makes brief interventions, privileging public debate over weighty formal pronouncements.

To be a sociologist, Becker says, is not to be an administrator, the adviser to a prince, an expert journalist, or a union representative for the careers of one's colleagues. You cannot be a manager and an activist at the same time. He never employs people on his own research projects. He does not pay for any assistants, has never had a secretary or a secretariat (other than the general office support for a whole department), and does not benefit from the structures of any research group or public funding. He is a pure craft worker. He treats colleagues and students alike, citing and using their results equally. In contrast to so many self-styled "deconstructionists," his sociology is subversive not because he rehabilitates common sense – although he does not disdain this – but because he creates a form of popular science directed to a wider public.

The aspiration to disseminate one's work beyond academic circles is frequently heard. There are as many kinds of sociology as there are sociologists: they all want to reach the public at large. However, these "currents" or "schools" depend for their credibility on their access to power and their institutional positions, rather than on the substance of their evidence and arguments. Their legitimacy comes only from their official status and authority, which is why the power struggles within sociology can be more vicious than elsewhere. The consequences should concern French sociology, which is particularly vulnerable to them.

Rejection of Academicism

We often find Becker in unexpected places. These raise questions that he has long reflected upon and mulled over, about the possible shape of the discipline. The experience of a narrow program delivered by a cadre of junior instructors, that would be typical for a graduate from an elite university,[4] deserves to be criticized. This model gives concrete expression to the academicism of the social sciences in France. It distorts their creative independence and their freedom of writing. It fixes a hierarchy of problem agendas, freezing specialties in ritualized forms of teaching, and the production of textbooks, dictionaries and commentaries. The result is a monstrous heap of "theories," which increases every year with further studies of the classics or the "founding fathers," to the detriment of innovative research. To build a good career, publishable sociology means writing commercially successful pamphlets, recycling previous theoretical schemes, and adopting a false, bookish rationality rather than investigating a new topic. This is why I have not written yet another conventional textbook. Becker's work does not fit very well into that format: he should not be read in a summary version, to tick a box or satisfy a dissertation requirement.

All the social sciences – not just sociology – are touched by the need for young people to invest in career strategies that will create what is supposed to be the best possible profile for self-advancement. This is obvious when we read about their fear of sanctions from application screeners and recruitment panels. Young people are trained to make polite references, to respect traditions and to conform when they naturally are, or should be, boldly challenged by the questions that arise for their, new, generation. Throughout the dissertation defenses or presentations in which I have participated, I have been saddened by the way students have been discouraged from departing from tradition and expected to adopt docility as a principle for survival. We should not dismiss the benefits that were formerly produced, by the education of an elite at the "Normale Sup.," first at Ulm and then at Cachan (but not exclusively or completely achieved there).[5] However, these benefits were quickly limited by the inflexibility of a curriculum that was too prescriptive to accommodate sociology. This is a discipline that is informal, incomplete and critical of the established order. It is held back by excessively rigid institutionalization.

The attempt to define a fixed, weighty and cumulative body of knowledge, and supposedly rigorous ways of thinking about it, introduced by the dual organization of the *École Normale* (study in different faculties and institutions, the *agrégation*)[6] has devastated the discipline. Even the slight benefits that a cloistered elite might derive from sociology have been lost. Sociology has nothing to gain from being made to fit the ENS template. It cannot, then, become a proper member of that school. Today, recruitment, education and training in the craft of sociology face several contradictory pressures, where one loses as others gain. This is evident in the decline, if not the collapse, of staffing and publications. The learning from experience advocated by Becker, tinged by the pragmatism of William James and Charles S. Peirce, rejects the cumulation of knowledge through books, an apprenticeship that fosters a muddled style of writing, in order to pass examinations. The smartest and most skillful students, in social terms, are not bad at adopting and reproducing a kind of superficial brilliance. They learn ways of working that are actually detrimental to developing their own independence of thought, criticizing sacred traditions and equal to the task of creating knowledge fit for their own generation. This perpetuates a structure in French higher education that creates two tracks for students. Some are steered to success in the competition for honors, to excellence, and others, often from lower-class backgrounds, are left as a poorly educated mass. A divergence persists between the education offered by the *grandes écoles* and that by the ordinary universities. I have experienced this contrast as a teacher. It reproduces an artificial culture of elitist learning: success in academic competition is judged by the quantity of knowledge that has been acquired rather than by inventiveness in its application. This is why social ingenuity, adaptation to difficult sites, practical skills or ethnographic daring are poorly understood and not taught. The elimination of the adventurous and original part of research is the consequence of an education that encourages mindless repetition, the ability to read quickly and exclusive ownership of ideas. Becker has always been the enemy of such distortions.

It will be clear that I am an admirer of Becker, although not an unconditional one, despite being separated in age, education, and certainly in the scale and value of our academic works. My present commentary should be read as an insight into the fundamental differences between our two countries. The definition of sociology, the methods used, and the historical depth of the American experience (where sociology was institutionalized in universities around 1890, about eighty years before this happened in France)[7] means that our big cousin has long operated with the confidence that comes from the scale of its influence throughout the anglophone world, with which we cannot compete.

I have praised Becker's emancipatory approach, which opposes both disciplinary imperialism and the kinds of systems thinking in sociology known as structuralism. His attitude, as one who spins out new ideas, is the opposite of those who declare: "I have invested in a field, I have identified all the research agendas and I am not going anywhere else." That stance leads to misconceptions about the nature of sociological books. It produces authors who are poorly adapted to the requirements for publication (the commercial conditions that frame this, the need for a clear beginning and end, dealing with a topic that has been conceptually defined in advance by the society). The alternative is to try to join the privileged class whose publications are subsidized through a connection to the CNRS or other public research centers.[8] One day the profession will be called to account for this unjust discrimination. As things currently stand, they expose French readers to the risks of sociological errors.

The absence of certain problem agendas and the occasions when Becker's conceptions have been misunderstood should not surprise us. The issues of race, of industry, of the legal and the hidden economy, are missing, although they loom large in contemporary concerns. People of color are almost never discussed although the question of race relations was the touchstone of Robert Park's work.[9] Economic life is not one of Becker's strengths. He rejects these themes as too general and too ill-defined to be dealt with through ethnography. Moreover, he does not know them well enough from the inside to venture into such densely populated territory. In reading Becker, we need both to assess him within his national context and to recognize how much we have underestimated empirical American sociology.

For some of us, working within a team has helped to avoid these obstacles. Jean-Pierre Briand, Jean-Michel Chapoulie, and Henri Peretz, from the University of Paris VIII-Vincennes have hosted, translated and introduced several American sociologists, all trained by, or associated with, Everett Hughes.[10] A collection within that university's library has been created in his honor. In this way, we escaped the confrontation with Marxism in the form of Bourdieu's inescapable determinism. This still stirs the passions of sociologists but that debate seemed sterile to us. We looked for a more empirical approach (fieldwork, participant observation, critical of the unreflective use of statistics), which we found in the work of the Chicago School. This pathway was rich in ideas (a sociology of interviews, interactions, life histories), and non-dogmatic. The approach appealed to us because it did not try to police its boundaries and exclude people.

Professional recognition of Howard Becker in our country began around 1985 with the publication of *Outsiders*. This has become a key work of reference thanks to a remarkable translation and persuasive introduction by his first advocates, Jean-Pierre Briand and Jean-Michel Chapoulie. Over the subsequent twenty-five years, a second and a third team of translators has engaged with his work. Several different groups have consolidated around his thinking: in Paris, Raymonde Moulin and Pierre-Michel Menger; in Grenoble, Alain Pessin and Alain Blanc; in Marseilles, Alain Guillemin and Jean-Claude Passeron. We can add the Swiss translators of *Sociological Work*, led by Marc-Henry Soulet. Becker's publications have been shared between six publishers (Métailié, La Découverte, Flammarion, l'Harmattan, Economica, Presses de Fribourg). This is the opposite of the introduction of Erving Goffman whose work has benefited (or possibly suffered) from having a single promoter in Pierre Bourdieu and a single publisher, leading to a more standardized approach.

Becker's impact has followed a similarly unusual course. He has been awarded four honorary doctorates (Paris VIII, Grenoble, Lyon-ETS, CNAM Paris). If we look at the places where he has been invited to present his work in conferences or seminars or to sit on juries, however, these are all in the east of the country. Nowhere else (with the exception of Paris)! From Metz and Nancy to Aix-Marseilles by way of Lyon and Grenoble, he has been invited to present. But nothing from Lille to Toulouse and the whole of the west. It is as if France is divided in two on the subject. This strange geography is matched by that of the sales of his work or the juries in which he has participated, leading us to think that, at least for students, their reading lists or their professors' work are matters of chance or geographical contingency. Becker's reception in other European countries has been equally skewed. Some countries rate him highly while others treat his work with total indifference. These are mysteries of the flow of ideas, as impenetrable as the ways of God!

As we have already seen, Becker's approach was initially seen as an alternative in the eyes of those who wanted to carry out research that did not rely on official statistics or survey questionnaires (Masson 2008, pp. 192–202). His "discovery" in France was part of the wider interest in the Chicago School. Since then, our understanding of "American" sociology has been enlarged to include a number of other authors, extending across other branches or currents. Our access to this sociology now allows us to recognize the merits of the syntheses of pragmatism or ethnography that Daniel Céfaï (2003, 2010) has set out in his recent introductions and presentations.

Becker's accessibility and frequent visits to France have contributed to his reception. His affection for France has made our country his third country of choice (after his home country and Brazil, where he has also spent time). One of the reasons is the many friendships that he has established: Raymonde Moulin, Pierre-Michel Menger, Jean-Claude Passeron, Dominique Pasquier, Sabine Chal-von-Demersay, Alain Pessin, Catherine Dutheil-Pessin, Alain Blanc, Bruno Latour and Antoine Hennion, Bruno Péquignot, Alain Garrigou, Florence Deloche-Gaudez, Jean-Yves Trépos, and Pierre Tripier, without forgetting Jean-Pierre Briand, Jean-Michel Chapoulie and Henri Peretz and other "fellow-travellers." His simple encouragements – he never implies "I know it all, I will tell you the direction to take" – are accepted. He also freely acknowledges his own intellectual debts. He has said how much he has learned from reading Raymonde Moulin, Bruno Latour or Antoine Hennion.

His detractors accuse him, without saying so openly, of presenting sociology as a practice that may be ill-defined in advance, open to non-professional influences, and capable of being carried on outside the academy. Such a stance seems like a heresy in our country of *Grandes Écoles* and defenders of an armchair version of sociology. It is true that his approach explicitly opposes elitism. The same goes for his iconoclasm about the proper way of doing social commentary. This is why *Outsiders* and *Art Worlds* were his greatest successes in France – because of the extent to which they were read outside our discipline. The reception of these two works divided specialists in epistemology and in art, spaces where French sociologists were active in some numbers and, consequently, were particularly sensitive to the challenge. His influence is reflected in a book of tributes offered by French sociologists under the leadership of Alain Pessin and Alain Blanc (2004), where five out of the ten chapters discuss Becker's approach to art.

Sociologists of work, and of professions less concerned with aesthetic issues, read Becker's work rather later and found it less attractive. He has been considered as an author of original, but atypical, ideas by the disciples of Alain Touraine and Michel Crozier.[11] He has been dismissed by both rational choice methodologists and by neo-Marxists. Certainly, Becker does not aspire to save humanity every day of the week. Not having ideas about everything; not having an answer to every question; not being concerned with every problem; not responding to critics: perhaps this is the beginning of sociological wisdom. Nevertheless, he is accepted and valued because he speaks for a renowned institution – the University of Chicago. He has worked at the highest level since his student days. He has long been exposed to international currents in the home of Thomas, Park, and Hughes. The Chicago School was open to the world and its students were encouraged to travel. Polish peasants or Japanese immigrants, East European religious minorities in the USA, the Jews of Frankfurt, the Chinese – all these were familiar topics for its students (especially those of Park or Dewey, who both knew China well). When Becker, as they did, made a visit to teach, whether in Brazil or in France, he committed himself to learn the language, and to become familiar with the history and the culture. These were not simply professional journeys but cultural experiences. For a dozen years, he has made an annual visit to our country, spending several months here and taking part in many conferences and juries, as well as being a tireless reader, travelling across the boundaries of national traditions.

The reservations that he arouses do not concern the right position to take in relation to American sociology or on the subject of the Chicago School and the myths that have grown up around it. The English sociologists, Jennifer Platt (1996) and Martin Bulmer (1984), have written detailed and critical perspectives on the history, as has Andrew Abbott (1999). They have improved our knowledge of the sociology department and given us a particular understanding of its approach to ethnography, which Becker has chosen not to discuss. In the same way, he sees no need to justify the temporal or thematic limits of his studies: it is sometimes disappointing that he goes so quickly through his introductory statements. He does not waste time on polemics, although his detractors, the anti ethnographers or the hyper-analytic crowd, would say that he does not sufficiently "define" his topics in advance.

Each new published work makes Becker more and more unclassifiable. What specialization, what body of knowledge has he created? Is he doing an analysis of media, a sociology of knowledge or a study of communication? Is he developing a program for the sociology of science? He describes himself as a realist sociologist, sometimes as a geographer or a photographer. This is not the core of his approach. It would be easy for him to retort that he is no different from Erving Goffman, a friend since their student days in Chicago. Despite the piecemeal nature of his writings, Becker remains within the Cartesian tradition. His novel contribution may be his emphasis on the dispersion and uncertainty of judgments as inescapable conditions in the construction of all our criteria. Finally, he has offended European sociologists by his indifference to Marxism and to economic factors. He does not directly explain his avoidance of "hot topics" – globalization, race, class, exploitation! He says: "Yes, I do leave those aside, but where is my material? The working class – I was not born into it but I do know about the middle classes! So, I work with the materials to hand. I have observed their expansion and the growth in leisure time; and I foresaw the elimination of barriers between public and private life and the permanent display of the self." He can justly claim: "The material determinants of sociology and its organizational environments, the struggle against the ideology of scientism, it seems to me that I have led that struggle!" And he would be right.

It is not unusual for an author to contribute to more than one field: non-specialization is a talent. But Becker goes further. He seems to reject altogether the idea of uniformity in his own work, to refuse to set out a unique direction, let alone to talk about a research program, to create a distinctive theory or to train disciples or courtiers, all things that he loathes. At Chicago, are the third and fourth generations fed up with the "School"? Is Becker locked into a fever of activity, untroubled by the reception of his work among those who prefer formal consistency? Certainly not. But he shows himself through so many activities – photos, visual sociology, exhibitions, theatre, music, books – in dizzying profusion. So many approaches! So many start-ups and initiatives! Is he a brilliant jack-of-all-trades or just endlessly dissatisfied? That is a false antithesis. In Professor Becker's store, you can find everything. You are just as likely to come across something that is ready-to-wear as a kit to assemble yourself. Let yourself go! What are the hidden goals? Being ready to work by instinct, intuition or curiosity? The constant movement of a lively spirit? Flitting around, jumping from one subject to another, avoiding linkages or connections between books, these are the product of a fluid approach, a flexible spirit. The work of research comes first! Always and again! This seems convincing, even though he would recognize that arguments are sometimes a source of clarification and that confrontation can take debates forward. However, you must understand that Becker continues to follow the path of an untroubled innovator, as he has done for as long as I have known him.

I met Becker on various occasions between 1981 and 1985, when I visited some of the most prominent representatives of empirical American sociology. He was at the head of my list when I saw him and he encouraged me to meet the colleagues that he thought were most interesting. Through him, I encountered Egon Bittner, Herbert Blumer, Ruth Cavan, Aaron Cicourel, Arlene Daniels, Fred Davis, Irwin Deutscher, Eliot Freidson, Joseph Gusfield, Ruth Horowitz, Everett Hughes, Moris Janowitz, Helena Lopata Znaniecki, David Riesman, Julius Roth, Anselm Strauss, Charles Tilly, Ralph Turner, Robert Weiss, and William Foote Whyte. I was introduced to a vast network of friends. I was touched by their welcome and the warmth of their reception for an obscure French scholar who had hardly published anything and had no letter of recommendation. I was also able to get together with the only French member of the Chicago School, Paule Verdet, who had "fled" Paris to study with Hughes in the 1950s. Everyone found time to record an interview with me, either at home or in their office. They replied to my questions in a straightforward way, treating me as an equal in terms that were quite amazing to someone who was accustomed to hierarchy and class structures within the world of scholarship. Their open-mindedness (they asked me as many questions about my country and my work as I asked them) was more than just politeness. They showed an authentically democratic feeling, proving to me that sociology could be a great opportunity for human connections.

Sociology practiced through observation, in its broadest sense, develops a heightened level of curiosity about everything that happens in society. It allows us to escape premature specialization, the weight of theory, obscurity. Everything that my colleagues and I have tried to make happen in France. Let us learn a final lesson about the intellectual value of sources drawn from outside the discipline, texts from the heart of the wider culture, allied to a direct knowledge of the social world, acquired outside offices or libraries. If we look at Becker's footnotes and sources, we can estimate that only 10 percent correspond to the norms that are usually expected and practiced. What does he put in their place? Personal testimonies, the outputs of various sciences (while still keeping psychology at a distance), his own informal observations and above all the fruits of his extensive reading of authors who excel at description, especially in literature. No matter that only ten professional sociologists are cited out of a hundred authors whose work he finds interesting. "So what," he would reply. "It's not a big deal, take advantage of what's out there. If I have not respected sacred texts, do the same. I have shown you the way!" His iconoclastic argument is unstoppable: he does not acknowledge any special supremacy or exclusive property rights in methodology or sociological inquiry. With his conviction that social change is permanent, he calls only for caution and modesty in our claims for "results."

He has shown this throughout a career that is still yet to be completed. He has the courage to be cautious, the originality of someone who is quite conformist in his everyday life, the audacity to be modest. Truly an involuntary revolutionary? Sometimes it is the fear of adventure that drives great adventurers and everyday routine that creates the ferment of ideas that disrupt it. Of course, no one is perfect: in Becker's store, there are some customers who are dissatisfied and others who are indifferent to the goods on offer. Moreover, all this is anecdotal. Driving ambition can confront a hostile social response. A burning desire for fame sometimes conceals a desire for domination at any price. Is that what motivates Becker? No. It is the passion for research, the need to understand and to share, that lies at the roots of an exceptional intellectual productivity that has been sustained and renewed for seventy years. This is a biological phenomenon and an astonishing social event. Is Becker falsely modest? I do not think so! Rather, humble! Above all it is a kind of "madness for sociology" as he puts it.

Let us acknowledge, then, his taste for craftsmanship, the extraordinary amount of time that he has devoted to the task and the scale of his output. I think he is telling us that, in order to advance, it is not necessary to first step backwards.

Constantly returning to the past by means of concealed autobiographies, repeatedly explaining oneself, these are a waste of time and prevent us from moving forward. Certainly, there is a danger that others will fail to understand his refusal to engage in intellectual introspection as far as explaining the work in its own terms. Is this a lack of ego or Olympian wisdom? Shame or fear? In any case, I say again, he has the courage to refuse to engage. His absence of belief in the unity or the coherence of a body of work that is always being reconstructed, never finished in spirit or in the minds of his readers, can be explained by an interactionist's sensitivity to the collective and changing conditions of creative work. When one asks the question, he declines to reply or simply says "that's how it is." This is why his work is so misunderstood by readers who are in a hurry or looking to apply a label. For others, it is a matter for infinite reflection and constant reinvigoration.

Notes

1 In a personal communication, Becker notes that he was never actually a candidate. He refused to accept an invitation to run for the office – American Sociological Association rules require that two candidates are nominated so that elections are always contested. He quotes a friend as saying, "If you lose it's a scandal and if you win it's a catastrophe!" According to Becker, Goffman accepted the nomination, which he didn't want, because, as he said, "A man has to do what he has to do." He was seriously ill with stomach cancer at the time and died shortly after the end of his term of office. See also Huber (2009).

2 Becker was the first editor of Symbolic Interaction (1977–1978). Peneff is referring here to the pattern, which is more common in Europe, of a leading scholar editing a journal for a long period of time and using this position to promote the work of their colleagues and graduate students.

3 Peneff is referring here to the expectation in France that a certain kind of intellectual will appear regularly on late night chat shows. This is a media format that is not commonly found elsewhere. It does involve a certain amount of ritual combat between scholars taking opposed public stances on social, economic, cultural or political issues, often with a studio audience. However, it is not intended as light entertainment of the kind more commonly found in the anglophone world. Becker could not reasonably be described as media-shy – he has been the subject of a substantial profile (Gopnik 2015) in the *New Yorker*, for example – but has not actively courted publicity for himself or his work.

4 The original text has "Normalien–Scolaire". A "normalien" is a graduate from the *École Normale Supérieure* – see Chapter 2, Note 3.

5 The original *École Normale Supérieure*, founded in 1794, is situated at the rue d'Ulm in the centre of Paris. A second *École Normale Supérieure* was developed from a technical education program in Paris, established in 1912. It has been located at Cachan, in the southern suburbs of Paris since 1957. There are two other similar institutions at Lyon and Rennes.

6 Peneff is referring here to the organizational complexity of the ENS. Students are recruited through different competitive routes – some from specialist high school tracks and some who have graduated from other universities. Courses and diplomas can be taken from other universities in the Paris area and students may also study for the *agrégation* – see Chapter 3, Note 3. The ENS has relatively few permanent, full-time faculty, relying heavily on external providers or joint appointments to deliver its own teaching.

7 Peneff is referring here to the expansion of sociology in France during the late 1950s and 1960s, after a long fallow period. Although the first French chair in sociology had been

established in 1885, held by Charles Letourneau at the *École d'Anthropologie de Paris*, there was very little institutional continuity. While Durkheim had attempted to develop a group of scholars, many of them were killed in World War I and he, himself, died in 1917 (Fournier 2013). This context is discussed more fully in my introduction.

8 The greater institutional separation between research and teaching in France means that many research-active academics depend upon a connection to a research center for access to resources. These do not automatically flow through their substantive university position. Among those resources are publication and translation subsidies, intended to promote French scholarship. These are a basis for patronage so that what appears in print, or in other languages, may reflect the preferences and networks of powerful individuals rather than representing the best or most current work in the field.

9 This may understate Becker's interest in issues of race. In various places, including an interview with Bourmeau and Heurtin (1997), he refers to the influence of *Black Metropolis* (Drake and Cayton 2015), which was first published in 1945, on his decision to study sociology rather than literature in graduate school. Drake (1911–1990) became a leading Black academic sociologist, while Cayton (1903–1970) worked mainly outside universities. This book is a historical and ethnographic study of the African-American experience in Chicago, from a project directed by Lloyd Warner (Peretz 2004). As such, it was describing a community that Becker would necessarily have been very familiar with from his other career as a jazz musician. The book has an introduction by Cayton's friend, Richard Wright (1908–1960), a pioneering Black radical writer. Wright lived in Chicago 1927–37, before moving to New York and finally settling in Paris in 1946. The blend of history, ethnography and literature is very characteristic of Becker's own work (see Becker 2007a).

10 Becker suggests that the contributions of Daniel Céfaï (EHESS) and Isaac Joseph (Paris X) should also be mentioned here.

11 Alain Touraine (1925–) and Michel Crozier (1922–2013) were leading figures in the development of French research on work and organizations during the 1950s and 1960s. They played important roles in the institutional development of French sociology in the 1960s and trained many contemporary leaders.

CONCLUSION

Becker represents continuity in the movement of ideas across almost a hundred years and four generations: from Thomas to Park, from Park to Hughes, from Hughes to Becker and his contemporaries, and finally to their current successors. Because Becker considers himself a simple link in a long history, he has been one of its most creative contributors. He is one of the principal exemplars of the loosely bounded movement known as Chicago sociology. At the turn of this century he became its torchbearer. His attitude is a valuable lesson. Sociology is currently misusing its cultural visibility. It suffers from a sickness of power, a desire to be featured in mass media, and a passion to be notorious.

We asked at the start of this exercise "Why should we read Howard Becker?" We now have our answer: to free us from fixed frameworks of thought, to push back against academicism in all its varied forms with their insidious hierarchies, castes and fake knowledge; to abolish the sects and the Schools, eliminating barriers or codes that are too strict, methodological principles that are rigid; above all to "de-psychologize" sociology, a constant danger that is particularly formidable today. He serves this purpose – and calls out to those who will listen, "Liberate the social."

In spite of everything, Becker remains a calm man, particularly in contrast to our many frantic colleagues. We can understand his refusal to engage in public life under the banner of his profession, his scientific skepticism in regard to armchair militancy or petition-signing. His disdain for ideology is accepted. We may perhaps retort to those who resist this position that there are appropriate contributions, a balance to be struck in the use of sociology in public life. A researcher can live in the anonymity of an activist within a crowd while maintaining neutrality in their professional life. These are not incompatible. It is one of the innumerable divisions of the personality that are required by human institutions.

It remains that sociology according to Becker should be fun and stimulating, a game: its style should be engaging, each small part played as brightly as a piece of music. Since Becker talks of jazz and uses it as a metaphor, let us do the same in our turn. Society is like an orchestra. The interactions in jazz are immediate: one player responds to another. All of them play to interpret a precedent, which prompts an idea, an agreement and an action – "you have taken up this key, this rhythm, so I will respond in tune – or perhaps not." The same principle is the basis of collective action. The musical example helps us to grasp the part played by improvisation in social life. Whatever our chosen objective, we take up the theme of the melody and argue with it, while maintaining the tempo or the figure with an element of innovation. Learning sociology while playing jazz was a great opportunity for Becker. We can immediately understand specific and fleeting communities (the band for the evening) where each member respects the general line but must also add their grain of inspiration. What a great lesson to learn. It is the reason why I have linked Becker's two great passions in the title of this book.

From the fertile ground of jazz music, Becker, having played his solo part, says to you: "Young people, here it is. I have contributed my chorus. What are you going to play now?" If you have a question to ask, put it to him: "Howie, what should we do? How should we practice sociology according to your example?" And he will certainly reply: "Do as much fieldwork as you can, build your confidence, take your professional future into your own hands – it's up to you to find out." Then open the window and listen to him playing his "Swinging Piano Jazz."

REFERENCES

Abbott, A. 1999. *Department and discipline: Chicago sociology at one hundred*. Chicago: University of Chicago Press.

Allemand, S. 1998. Où en est l'école de Chicago? *Sciences Humaines* No. 85 (July) https://www.scienceshumaines.com/ou-en-est-l-ecole-de-chicago_fr_10081.html [accessed January 30, 2018].

Aron, R. 1967. *Les étapes de la pensée sociologique*. Paris: Gallimard. (Translated as *Main currents in sociological thought*. New York: Basic Books, 1967.)

Atkinson, J.M. 1978. *Discovering suicide: studies in the social organization of sudden death*. London: Macmillan.

Becker, H.S. 1953. Field methods and techniques: A note on interviewing tactics. *Human organization*, 12(4), pp. 31–32.

Becker, H.S. ed. 1962. *The other side: perspectives on deviance*. New York: Free Press.

Becker, H.S. 1966. Whose side are we on? *Social Problems*, 14(3), pp. 239–247.

Becker, H.S. 1970. *Sociological work: method and substance*. Chicago: Aldine. (Translated as *Le travail sociologique: méthode et substance*. Fribourg: Academic Press Fribourg, 2006.)

Becker, H.S. 1972. A school is a lousy place to learn anything in. *American Behavioral Scientist*, 16(1), pp. 85–105.

Becker, H.S. 1974. Photography and sociology. *Studies in the Anthropology of Visual Communication* 1(1), pp. 3–26.

Becker, H.S. 1979. What's happening to sociology? *Society*, 16 (July-August), pp. 19–24.

Becker, H.S. 1981. *Exploring society photographically*. Evanston, IL: Mary and Leigh Block Gallery.

Becker, H.S. 1982. *Art worlds*. Berkeley, CA: University of California Press.

Becker, H.S. 1986. *Doing things together: selected papers*. Evanston, IL: Northwestern University Press.

Becker, H.S. 1996. *The epistemology of qualitative research*. In: Jessor, R., Colby, A. and Schweder, R. eds., *Essays on ethnography and human development*. Chicago: University of Chicago Press, pp. 53–71.

Becker, H.S. 1998. *Tricks of the trade: how to think about your research while you're doing it*. Chicago: University of Chicago Press. (Translated as *Les ficelles du metier: Comment conduire sa recherche en sciences sociales*. Paris: La Découverte, 2002.)

Becker, H.S. 2007. Preface. http://howardsbecker.com/articles/dictionaire.html [accessed January 30, 2018] (Originally published as Préface. In: Le Digol, C. éd. *Dictionnaire de sociologie*. Paris: Albin Michel/Encyclopaedia Universalis).

Becker, H.S. 2007a. *Telling about society*. Chicago: University of Chicago Press. (Translated as *Comment parler de la societé: artistes, écrivains, chercheurs et représentations sociales*. Paris: La Découverte, 2009.)

Becker, H.S. 2007b. *Writing for social scientists: how to start and finish your thesis, book, or article.* 2nd ed. Chicago: University of Chicago Press. (1st ed.1986.)

Becker, H.S. 2008. *Outsiders*. 2nd ed. New York: Simon and Schuster. (1st ed.New York: Free Press, 1963.)

Becker, H.S. 2009a. Learning to observe in Chicago. http://howardsbecker.com/articles/observe.html [accessed January 30, 2018] (Originally published as 'Grandir et observer à Chicago'. In: Peneff, J. *Le goût de l'observation Comprendre et pratiquer l'observation participante en sciences sociales*. Paris: La Découverte, pp. 60–61, 76–77 and 126–127.)

Becker, H.S. 2009b. How to find out how to do qualitative research. http://howardsbecker.com/articles/NSF.html [accessed January 30, 2018].

Becker, H.S. 2012. The art of not doing fieldwork: Maurice Halbwachs' failed encounter with the Chicago School. *Books & Ideas.net*. September 5. http://www.booksandideas.net/The-Art-of-Not-Doing-Fieldwork.html [accessed January 30, 2018].

Becker, H.S. 2014. *What about Mozart? What about Murder? Reasoning from cases*. Chicago: University of Chicago Press.

Becker, H.S. 2017. *Evidence*. Chicago: University of Chicago Press.

Becker, H.S. and Pessin, A. 2017. Appendix A: a dialogue on the ideas of "world" and "field". In: Pessin, A. *The sociology of Howard S. Becker: theory with a wide horizon*. Chicago: University of Chicago Press, pp. 91–104. (Originally published as Becker, H.S. and Pessin, A. 2006. Dialogue sure les notions de "monde" et "champ". *Sociologie de l'Art*. 8, pp. 165–180. Translation by H.S. Becker first published 2006 in *Sociological Forum* 21(2), pp. 275–286.)

Becker, H.S., Geer, B. and Hughes, E.C. 1968. *Making the grade: the academic side of college life*. New York: Wiley. (2nd ed., with new introduction by H.S. Becker, New Brunswick, NJ: Transaction, 1995.)

Becker, H.S., Geer, B., Hughes, E.C. and Strauss, A. L. 1961. *Boys in white: student culture in medical school*. Chicago: University of Chicago Press.

Berrebi-Hoffmann, I. and Grémion, P. 2009. Élites intellectuelles et réforme de l'état: esquisse en trois temps d'un déplacement d'expertise . *Cahiers Internationaux de Sociologie*, 2009/1 n° 126, pp. 39–59.

Bourdieu, P., 1977. *Outline of a theory of practice* (Cambridge Studies in Social Anthropology 16). Cambridge: Cambridge University Press. (Originally published as *Esquisse d'une théorie de la pratique*. Geneva: Droz, 1972.)

Bourdieu, P. 1979. *La distinction: critique sociale du jugement*. Paris: Éditions de Minuit. (Translated as *Distinction: a social critique of the judgement of taste*. Cambridge, MA: Harvard University Press, 1984.)

Bourdieu, P., 1985. The genesis of the concepts of habitus and field. *Sociocriticism*, 2(2), pp. 11–24.

Bourdieu, P. 1986. The forms of capital. In: Richardson, J. ed. *Handbook of theory and research for the sociology of education*. New York: Greenwood, pp. 225–239. (Originally published as "Ökonomisches Kapital, kulturelles Kapital, soziales Kapital." In: Kreckel, R. ed. *Soziale Ungleichheiten* (Soziale Welt, Sonderheft 2). Goettingen: Otto Schwarz & Co., 1983. pp. 183–198.)

Bourdieu, P. ed. 1999. *The weight of the world: social suffering in contemporary society*. Cambridge: Polity. (Originally published as *La Misère du monde*. Paris: Éditions du Seuil, 1993.)

Bourdieu, P. and Passeron, J.-C. 1964. *Les héritiers: les étudiants et la culture.* Paris: Éditions de Minuit.

Bourmeau, S. and Heurtin, J.-P. 1997. La carrière déviante du professeur Becker: de Al Jolson à Georges Perec (en passant par Everett Hughes). *Politix* 10(37), pp. 155–166. http://www.persee.fr/doc/polix_0295-2319_1997_num_10_37_1656 [accessed January 30, 2018].

Briand, J.-P. and Chapoulie, J.-M. 1992. *Les collèges du people: L'enseignement primaire supérieur et le développement de la scolarisation prolongée sous la Troisième République.* Lyon: ENS Éditions.

Briand, J.-P. and Peretz, H. eds. 1996. *Hommage à Howard S. Becker.* Paris: Université Paris 8.

Bulmer, M. 1984. *The Chicago School of sociology: institutionalization, diversity, and the rise of sociological research.* Chicago: University of Chicago Press.

Burawoy, M. 2002. Election Statement, 2002–2003 Candidates Announced for ASA Officers. *ASA Footnotes* March, p. 7.

Burawoy, M. 2005a. For public sociology. *American Sociological Review*, 70(1), pp. 4–28.

Burawoy, M. 2005b. The critical turn to public sociology. *Critical Sociology*, 31(3), pp. 313–326.

Burawoy, M. 2014. Sociology as a vocation: moral commitment and scientific imagination. *Current Sociology*, 62(2), pp. 279–284.

Céfaï, D. 2003. *L'Enquête de terrain.* Paris: La Découverte, 2003.

Céfaï, D. ed. 2010. *L'engagement ethnographique.* Paris: Éditions de l'École des hautes études en sciences sociales.

Chapoulie, J.-M. 1991. La seconde fondation de la sociologie française, les Etats-Unis et la classe ouvrière. *Revue française de sociologie*, 32(3) (Jul.–Sep.), pp. 321–364.

Chapoulie, J.-M. 2001. *La tradition de Chicago 1892–1961.* Paris: Seuil.

Chapoulie, J.-M. 2008. Malentendus transatlantiques. La tradition de Chicago, Park et la sociologie française. *L'Homme*, No. 187/188, *Miroirs Transatlantiques* (Jul. – Dec.), pp. 223–246.

Chapoulie, J.-M. and Briand, J.-P. 2000. Enseigner le travail de terrain et l'observation: un témoignage sur une experience (1970–1985). *Genèses* 39, pp. 138–155. http://www.cairn.info/revue-geneses-2000-2-page-138.html [accessed January 30, 2018].

Chapoulie, J.-M. and Tripier, P. eds. 1998. *Actes du colloque franco-américain "L'école de Chicago, hier et aujourd'hui", 3–4 avril 1998.* Saint-Quentin-en-Yvelines: Université de Versailles-Saint-Quentin-en-Yvelines.

Chombart de Lauwe, P.-H. and Bertin, J. 1952. *Paris et l'agglomération parisienne.* Paris: Presses Universitaires de France.

Cicourel, A.V. 1964. *Method and Measurement in Sociology.* New York: Free Press.

Coulon, A. 1987. *L'ethnométhodologie.* Paris: Presses Universitaires de France.

Coulon, A. 1992. *L'École de Chicago.* Paris: Presses Universitaires de France.

Crozier, M. 2005. Interview with Dominique Vellin. *Gérer et Comprendre*, juin 2005, n°80 http://www.annales.org/gc/2005/gc80/004-007crozier.pdf [accessed January 30, 2018].

Dahrendorf, R. 1973. *Homo Sociologicus.* London: Routledge & Kegan Paul.

Demazière, D. 2015. Claude Dubar : l'hommage de D. Demazière. http://www.test-afs-socio.fr/drupal/node/4449 [accessed January 30, 2018].

Desrosières, A. 1993. *La politique des grands nombres: Histoire de la raison statistique.* Paris: La Découverte. (Translated as *The Politics of Large Numbers: A history of statistical reasoning.* Cambridge, MA: Harvard University Press, 1998.)

Diani, M. 1987. Howard Becker: un classique de la sociologie americaine. *Sociétés* 12, p. 40.

Dingwall, R. 1980. Ethics and ethnography . *Sociological Review* 28(4), pp. 871–891.

Dingwall, R. 1997. Accounts, interviews and observations. In: Miller, G. and Dingwall, R. eds. *Context and Method in Qualitative Research*, London: Sage, pp. 51–65.

Dingwall, R. 1999. Professions and social order in a global society. *International Review of Sociology* 9(1), pp. 131–140.

Dingwall, R. 2016. The ecological metaphor in the sociology of occupations and professions. In: Liljegren, A. and Saks, M. eds. *Professions and Metaphors: Understanding Professions in Society*. London: Routledge, pp.31–48.

Dingwall, R., and McDonnell, M.B. 2015. Conclusion. In: Dingwall, R. and McDonnell, M.B. eds. *Sage handbook of research management*. London: Sage, pp. 604–616.

Dingwall, R.Eekelaar, J.M. and Murray, T. 1983. *The Protection of Children: State Intervention and Family Life*. Oxford: Basil Blackwell (2nd edition, with new epilogue, Aldershot: Avebury, 1995.)

Diderot, D. 1964. *Quatre contes*. (edited by Proust, J.). Geneva: Droz.

Douglas, J.D. 1967. *The social meanings of suicide*. Princeton, NJ: Princeton University Press.

Drake, St C. and Cayton, Jr., H.R. 2015. *Black metropolis: a study of negro life in a northern city*. Chicago: University of Chicago Press. (First published New York: Harcourt Brace & Company, 1945.)

Drouard, A. 1982. Réflexions sur une chronologie: le développement des sciences sociales en France de 1945 à la fin des années soixante. *Revue Française de Sociologie* 23(1), pp. 55–85.

Durkheim, E. 1938. *The rules of sociological method*. New York: Free Press (Originally published as *Les règles de la méthode sociologique*. Paris: Félix Alcan, 1895.)

Durkheim, E. 1952. *Suicide: a study in sociology*. London: Routledge & Kegan Paul. (Originally published as *Le suicide*. Paris: Félix Alcan, 1897.)

Durkheim, E. 1995. *The Elementary Forms of Religious Life*. New York: Free Press. (Originally published as *Les Formes élémentaires de la vie religieuse: le système totémique en Australie*. Paris: Félix Alcan, 1912.)

El Miri, M. and Masson, P. 2009. Vers une juridicisation des sciences sociales? Sur l'utilité d'une charte de déontologie en sociologie. http://www.laviedesidees.fr/Vers-une-juridicisation-des.html [accessed January 30, 2018].

Faulkner, R. R. and Becker, H.S. 2009. *"Do you know…?" The jazz repertoire in action*. Chicago: University of Chicago Press.

Fine, G. ed. 1995. *A second Chicago School: the development of a postwar American sociology*. Chicago: University of Chicago Press.

Fitzi, G. and Marcucci, M. 2017. Durkheim in Germany: The performance of a classic. *Journal of Classical Sociology* 17(4), pp. 271–275.

Fournier, M. 2013. *Émile Durkheim: A Biography*. Cambridge: Polity. (Originally published as *Émile Durkheim*. Paris: Librairie Arthème Fayard, 2007.)

Freidson, E. 1985. *La profession médicale*. Paris: Payot (Originally published as *Profession of Medicine*. New York: Dodd Mead, 1970).

Garfinkel, H. 1956. Some sociological concepts and methods for psychiatrists. *Psychiatric Research Reports* 6, pp. 181–195.

Gerhardt, U. 1999. A world from brave to new: Talcott Parsons and the war effort at Harvard University. *Journal of the History of the Behavioral Sciences* 35(3), pp. 257–289.

Glaser, B.G. and Strauss, A.L. 1967. *The discovery of grounded theory*. Chicago: Aldine (Translated as *La découverte de la théorie ancrée. Stratégies pour la recherche qualitative*, Paris: Armand Colin, 2010.)

Goffman, E. 1968. *Asiles: Études sur la condition sociale des maladies mentaux*. Paris: Éditions de Minuit. (Originally published as *Asylums: essays on the social situation of mental patients and other inmates*. New York: Doubleday Anchor, 1961.)

Goffman, E. 1973. *La mise en scène de la vie quotidienne*. Paris: Éditions de Minuit. (Originally published as *The presentation of self in everyday life*. New York: Doubleday Anchor, 1959.)

Goffman, E. 1975, *Stigmates. Les usages sociaux des handicaps*. Paris: Éditions de Minuit. (Originally published as *Stigma: Notes on the management of spoiled identity*. Englewood Cliffs, NJ: Prentice Hall, 1964.)

Goffman, E., 1983. Felicity's condition. *American Journal of Sociology* 89(1), pp. 1–53.

Goldmann, L. 1964. *The hidden god: a study of tragic vision in the Pensées of Pascal and the tragedies of Racine*. London: Routledge & Kegan Paul. (Originally published as *Le dieu caché: etude sur la vision tragique dans le pensées de Pascal et dans le theatre de Racine*. Paris: Gallimard, 1955.)

Gonos, G. 1977. "Situation" versus "frame": the "interactionist" and the "structuralist" analyses of everyday life. *American Sociological Review* 42(6), pp. 854–867.

Goody, J.R. 2006. *The theft of history*. Cambridge: Cambridge University Press.

Gopnik, A. 2015. The outside game: how the sociologist Howard Becker studies the conventions of the unconventional. *The New Yorker*, January 12. https://www.newyorker.com/magazine/2015/01/12/outside-game [accessed January 30, 2018].

Grafmeyer, Y. and Joseph, I. 1979. *L'École de Chicago: naissance de l'écologie urbaine*. Paris: Éditions du Champ Urbain.

Grémion, P. 2005. From Pierre Bourdieu to Bourdieu. *Études: Revue de Culture Contemporaine* 402(1), pp. 39–53.

Gusfield, J. 1963. *Symbolic crusade: status politics and the American temperance movement*. Champaign, IL: University of Illinois Press.

Guth, S. 2000. *Fondation de la sociologie américaine : morceaux choisis*. Paris: L'Harmattan.

Halbwachs, M. 2012. *Écrits d'Amerique* (édition établie et presentée par Christian Topalov), Paris: Éditions de l'École des hautes études en sciences sociales.

Hatzfeld, N. 2002. *Les gens d'usine, 50 ans d'histoire à Peugeot–Sochaux*. Paris: Éditions de l' Atelier.

Histoires d'Universités. 2009. *L'illégitime CNU* 19 http://histoireuniversites.blog.lemonde.fr/2009/12/11/circulez-il-ny-a-rien/ [accessed January 30, 2018].

Hoare, Q. and Nowell Smith, G. 1971. *Selections from "The prison notebooks of Antonio Gramsci"*. London: Lawrence & Wishart.

Hobsbawm, E. 1998. *Uncommon People: Resistance, Rebellion and Jazz*. London: Weidenfeld & Nicolson. (Translated as *Rébellions: La résistance des gens ordinaires jazz, paysans et prolétaires*. Brussels: Editions Aden, 2011.)

Horowitz, I.L. and Liebowitz, M. 1968. Social deviance and political marginality: towards a redefinition of the relation between sociology and politics. *Social Problems* 15(3), pp. 280–296.

Huber, J. 2009. Erving Goffman's Presentation of Self as ASA President. *Bios Sociologicus: The Erving Goffman Archives*, http://digitalscholarship.unlv.edu/cgi/viewcontent.cgi?article=1036&context=goffman_archives [accessed January 30, 2018].

Hughes, E.C. 1971. *The sociological eye: selected papers*. Chicago: Aldine-Atherton.

Hughes, E.C., Hughes, H.M. and Deutscher, I. 1958. *Twenty thousand nurses tell their story: a report on the American Nurses Association studies of nursing functions*. Philadelphia: J.B. Lippincott.

INSEE (Institute national de la statistique et des études economiques). 2016. *Ethnic-based statistics*, https://www.insee.fr/en/information/2388586 [accessed January 30, 2018].

Lefebvre, H. 1969. *The Explosion: Marxism and the French Upheaval*. New York: Modern Reader. (Originally published as *L'irruption de Nanterre au sommet*. Paris: Éditions Anthropos, 1968.)

Lévy-Leblond, J.-M. 2010. *La science n'est pas l'art: Brèves rencontres…*Paris: Hermann.

Mandler, P. 2013. *Return from the natives: how Margaret Mead won the Second World War and lost the Cold War*. New Haven, CT: Yale University Press.

Lieberson, S., 1992. Einstein, Renoir, and Greeley: Some thoughts about evidence in Sociology: 1991 Presidential address. *American Sociological Review*, 57(1), pp. 1–15.

Marx, K. and Engels, F. 1968. *Selected Works*. London: Lawrence & Wishart.

Masson, P. 2008. *Faire de la sociologie: les grandes enquêtes françaises depuis 1945*. Paris: La Découverte.

Masson, P. and Schrecker, C. 2016. *Sociology in France after 1945*. Basingstoke: Palgrave Macmillan.

Mosbah-Natanson, S. 2008. Internationalisme et tradition nationale: le cas de la constitution de la sociologie française autour de 1900. *Revue d'histoire des sciences humaines*, 1, pp. 35–62.

Müller, A. 2009. *Howard Becker and Alain Mueller discuss "Telling about Society"* http://howardsbecker.com/articles/Suisse%20English.html (Originally published http://www.ethnographiques.org/2009/Becker-Muller) [both accessed January 30, 2018].

Oakeshott, M. 1991. On being conservative. In: Oakeshott, M. *Rationalism in Politics and Other Essays*. Indianapolis: Liberty Press, pp. 407–437. (First published London: Methuen, 1962).

Park, R.E. and Burgess, E.W. 1921. *Introduction to the Science of Sociology*. Chicago: University of Chicago Press.

Parsons, T. 1968. *The Structure of Social Action*. New York: Free Press (First published New York: McGraw-Hill, 1937).

Peneff, J. 1992. *L'Hôpital en urgence: étude par observation participante*. Paris: Métailié.

Peneff, J. 2004. Les idées originales d'Howard S. Becker pour enseigner la sociologie. In: Pessin, A. and Blanc, A. eds. *L'art du terrain: mélanges offerts à Howard Becker*. Paris: L'Harmattan, pp. 15–28.

Peneff, J. 2009. *Le goût de l'observation: comprendre et pratiquer l'observation participante en sciences sociales*. Paris: La Découverte.

Peretz, H. 2004. The making of *Black Metropolis*. *The Annals of the American Academy of Political and Social Science*, 595(1), pp. 168–175.

Pessin, A. 2017. *The sociology of Howard Becker: theory with a wide horizon*. Chicago: University of Chicago Press (Originally published as *Un sociologue en liberté: lecture de Howard Becker*. Québec City: Les Presses de l'Université Laval, 2004.)

Pessin, A. and Blanc, A. eds. 2004. *L'art du terrain: mélanges offerts à Howard Becker*. Paris: L'Harmattan.

Platt, J. 1996. *A history of sociological research methods in America 1920–1960*. Cambridge: Cambridge University Press.

Popper, K.R. 1961. *The Poverty of Historicism*. London: Routledge & Kegan Paul.

Ragin, C.C. and Becker, H.S. 1992. *What is a case? exploring the foundations of social inquiry*. Cambridge: Cambridge University Press.

Rousset, M. 2018. Pierre Bourdieu, cible et repère. *Le Monde*, 13 January.http://www.lemonde.fr/idees/article/2018/01/11/pierre-bourdieu-cible-et-repere_5240483_3232.html?xtmc=&xtcr=1 [accessed January 30, 2018].

Roy, D. 1952. Quota restriction and goldbricking in a machine shop. *American Journal of Sociology* 57(5), pp. 427–442.

Roy, D. 2006. *Un sociologue à l'usine*. Paris: La Découverte.

Shelley, P.B. 1840. In Defence of Poetry. In: Shelley, M. ed. *Essays, Letters from Abroad, Translations and Fragments*. London: Edward Moxon, pp. 1–57.

Simmel, G. 1950. The secret and the secret society. In: Wolff, K.H., ed. *The Sociology of Georg Simmel*. New York: Free Press, pp. 307–376.

Simon, J. 2004. Singing democracy: music and politics in Jean-Jacques Rousseau's thought. *Journal of the History of Ideas* 65(3), pp. 433–454.

Small, A.W. and Vincent, G.E. 1894. *An introduction to the study of society*. New York: American Book Company.

Strong, P.M. and Dingwall, R. 1989. Romantics and Stoics. In: Silverman, D. and Gubrium, J. eds. *The Politics of Field Research*. London: Sage, pp. 49–69.

Studholme, M. 1995. Durkheim and the institutionalization of British sociology. *Durkheimian Studies* 1(1), pp. 24–34.

Sutherland, E.H. 1937. *The professional thief*. Chicago: University of Chicago Press.

Touraine, A. 1977. *Un Désir d'histoire*. Paris: Stock.

Turner, J.H. 1984. Durkheim's and Spencer's principles of social organization: a theoretical note. *Sociological Perspectives* 27(1), pp. 21–32.

Vassy, C., Keller, R. C. and Dingwall, R. 2010. *Enregistrer les morts, identifier les surmortalités: une comparaison Angleterre, États-Unis et France*. Rennes: Presses de l'EHESP.

Vaughan, D. 1997. *The Challenger launch decision: risky technology, culture, and deviance at NASA*. Chicago: University of Chicago Press.

Verdet, P. 1997. Une française à l'école de Hughes. *Sociétés contemporaines* N°27, pp. 59–66. https://www.cairn.info/revue-societes-contemporaines-1997-3.htm [accessed January 30, 2018].

Weber, M. 1958. *The rational and social foundations of music*. Martindale, D., Riedel, J. and Neuwirth, G. eds. Carbondale, IL: Southern Illinois University Press. (Originally published as *Die rationalen und soziologischen Grundlagen der Musik*. Munich: Drei Masken Verlag, 1921).

Whyte, W. F. 1943. *Street corner society; the social structure of an Italian slum*. Chicago: University of Chicago Press. (Translated as *Street corner society: la structure sociale d'un quartier italo-américain*. Paris: La Découverte, 1996.)

Williams, R. 1976. *Keywords*. London: Fontana.

INDEX